YORK NOTES

D0192207

AQA UNSEEN POETRY

STUDY AND EXAM PRACTICE

MARY GREEN

Pearson

YORK PRESS

YORK PRESS
322 Old Brompton Road, London SW5 9JH

PEARSON EDUCATION LIMITED
Edinburgh Gate, Harlow,
Essex CM20 2JE, United Kingdom
Associated companies, branches and representatives throughout the world

First published 2017

10 9 8 7 6 5

ISBN 978–1–2921–8634–4

Typeset by DTP Media
Printed in Slovakia

Text credits: 'Text' from *Rapture* by Carol Ann Duffy. Published by Picador, 2008. Copyright © Carol Ann
Duffy. Reproduced by permission of the author c/o Rogers, Coleridge & White Ltd., 20 Powis Mews,
London W11 1JN. 'Salamander' by Mary Green reproduced by permission of the author. 'Installations'
by Mike Gould reproduced by permission of the author. 'Sea Bream Dinner' by Paul Deaton reproduced
by permission of the author and Seren Books. 'Green Thought' from *Rounding the Horn: Collected
Poems* by Jon Stallworthy (Carcanet Poetry, 1998) reproduced by permission of Carcanet Press Limited.
'Abra-Cadabra' from *I Have Crossed an Ocean: Selected Poems* by Grace Nichols (Bloodaxe Books, 2010).
Reproduced with permission of Bloodaxe Books. www.bloodaxebooks.com. Margaret Walker, 'Lineage'
from *This is My Century: New and Collected Poems*. Copyright © 1989 by Margaret Walker. Reprinted by
permission of University of Georgia Press. 'Canto CCCLXIV' by Niall O'Sullivan reproduced by permission
of the author. 'Piccadilly Line' from *Stitching the Dark: New & Selected Poems* by Carole Satyamurti
(Bloodaxe Books, 2005). Reproduced with permission of Bloodaxe Books. www.bloodaxebooks.com.
'The Letter' from *Ice* by Gillian Clarke (Carcanet Poetry, 2012) reproduced by permission of Carcanet
Press Limited. 'Moving' by John Pownall reproduced by permission of the author. 'Abandoned
Farmhouse' from *Sure Signs: New and Selected Poems*, by Ted Kooser, copyright © 1980. Reprinted by
permission of the University of Pittsburgh Press. 'Sally' from *The Leave Train: New and Selected Poems*
by Phoebe Hesketh reproduced by permission of Enitharmon Press.

Photo credits: Goldfaery/Shutterstock for page 7 bottom / © Runy Runge for page 9 margin / A & B
Photos/Shutterstock for page 10 / IriGri/Shutterstock for page 11 margin / samnooshka/© iStock for
page 12 / anopdesignstock/© iStock for page 13 margin / 4kclips/Shutterstock for page 14 margin /
tommystockphoto/© iStock for page 15 / Mark Caunt/Shutterstock for page 16 middle / johnnorth/
© iStock for page 16 bottom / Jacek Chabraszewski/© iStock for page 17 top /milicad/© iStock for page 18
bottom / Trong Nguyen/Shutterstock for page 22 bottom / turtix/© iStock for page 30 top / 501room/
© iStock for page 30 bottom / Catalin Petolea/Shutterstock for page 33 bottom / killerb10/© iStock for
page 35 bottom / Kevin Eaves/Shutterstock for page 37 bottom / Ed Phillips/© iStock for page 39 middle
/ idal/© iStock for page 41 bottom / ESB Professional/Shutterstock for page 55 bottom / kali9/© iStock for
page 57 bottom

CONTENTS

PART FOUR: SAMPLE PAPERS, ANSWERS AND PRACTICE TASKS

PART FIVE: LITERARY TERMS AND ANSWERS

PREPARING FOR ASSESSMENT

HOW WILL I BE ASSESSED ON MY ANSWER TO THE 'UNSEEN' POEMS?

When you answer the questions in **Section C** of your GCSE English Literature Paper 2, usually referred to as the 'unseen' poems, you will be examined on the following two Assessment Objectives:

Assessment Objectives	Wording	Worth thinking about ...
AO1	Read, understand and respond to texts. Students should be able to: • maintain a critical style and develop an informed response • use textual references, including quotations, to support and illustrate interpretations.	• Am I clear about what happens in the poems? • What do I think are the main ideas in the poems? • How can I make my views clear and convincing? • What are the key quotations and how can I use them to support my views?
AO2	Analyse the language, **form** and **structure** used by a writer to create meanings and effects, using relevant subject terminology where appropriate.	• What is the poet concerned about in the poem? What choices has he/she made? (For example, what does this image mean? How does the rhythm suit the feelings and ideas?) • What effects do the poet's choices create? Are they clear or **ambiguous**, optimistic or pessimistic?

Important: You do not have to show an understanding of the relationship between the unseen poems and the context in which they were written (**AO3**).

In other parts of your English Literature GCSE, **AO4**, which is related to spelling, punctuation and grammar, is also assessed. While you will not gain any marks for AO4 in your poetry examination, it is still important to ensure that you write accurately and clearly, in order to get your points across to the examiner in the best possible way.

Assessment Objectives **1** and **2** are about *what* poets do (the choices they make, and the effects these create), *what* your ideas are (your analysis and interpretation) and *how* you write about them (how well you explain your ideas).

> Look out for the Assessment Objective labels throughout this book. These will help to focus your study and revision.

ASSESSMENT OBJECTIVE 1

What does it say?	What does it mean?	Dos and don'ts
Read, understand and respond to texts. Students should be able to: ● Maintain a critical style and develop an informed personal response ● Use textual references, including quotations, to support and illustrate interpretations.	You must: ● Use some of the literary terms you have learned (correctly!) ● Write in a professional way (not a chatty way) ● Show that you have thought for yourself ● Back up your ideas with examples, including quotations	**Don't write:** *The salamander is like a puppet.* **Do write:** *The image of the salamander as a 'shadow puppet/Darting' suggests an energetic, playful creature whose shape is glimpsed only now and again.*

ASSESSMENT OBJECTIVE 2

What does it say?	What does it mean?	Dos and don'ts
Analyse the language, **form** and **structure** used by the poet to create meanings and effects, using relevant subject terminology where appropriate.	'Analyse' – comment **in detail** on **particular aspects** of the poem or language 'language' – what the poet writes and how they say it 'form' – **how** the poem is told (e.g. how the poem is laid out using different shapes or verse forms such as sonnet, quatrains, tercets) 'structure' – the **order** in which events are revealed, or in which characters appear, or descriptions are presented 'create meanings' – what can we, as readers, **infer** from what the poet tells us? What is **implied** by particular descriptions, or events? 'subject terminology' – **words** you should use when writing about poetry, such as imagery, metaphor, irony, symbol, setting, etc.	**Don't write:** *The poem is written in couplets.* **Do write:** *By writing the poem in the form of couplets the poet emphasises a series of images set apart from each other, giving the strong impression of pictures hanging in a gallery.*

INTRODUCTION TO PAPER 2, SECTION C: UNSEEN POETRY

After you have answered questions on the poems in the anthology cluster in Section B of Paper 2, you will be given two new poems in **Section C** that you have not seen before. These are referred to as the 'unseen' poems.

THE QUESTIONS

In Section C, there are two 'unseen' poems printed on the exam paper.

You will answer two essay-type questions.

QUESTION 1

This focuses on how the poet presents particular thoughts and ideas in the first poem. For example:

'How does the poet present the speaker's feelings about friendship?'

or

'How does the poet present the speaker's feelings about conflict?'

QUESTION 2

This asks you to compare an aspect of the two poems (find the similarities and differences). For example:

'In both poems the speakers describe feelings about seeing someone they love leave to fight in a war. What are the similarities and/or differences between the ways the poets present those feelings?'

> **TOP TIP** ★
>
> Allow yourself **at least 45 minutes** to answer questions on the 'unseen' poems. There are a couple more marks available for the 'unseen' poems (**32 marks**) than for the question on the anthology cluster in Section B (30 marks).

THE POEMS

The poems in Section C can be of any type so you need to make sure you are familiar with a range of poetry of different styles. When you read the poems, you should look for what seems to be special or **distinctive** about them and how the poet expresses this. It is rather like looking at a painting and thinking about what special quality it has and the materials the painter has chosen to accomplish it.

ASSESSMENT

There are 32 marks available for your answers on the 'unseen' poems:

Question	AO	Marks
1	AO1	12
	AO2	12
2	AO2	8

PART TWO: READING 'UNSEEN' POEMS

QUESTION 1 – THE FIRST UNSEEN POEM

READING THE POEM

When you read a poem for the first time allow yourself to respond to it simply, so that you have a rough idea of what the poem is about, rather than struggle to find specific or complicated meanings. Think about the **feelings** and **thoughts** the poem evokes in you.

On the second reading you can explore the **key techniques** the poet uses and the **effects** they create. Make sure you:

- are ready with an approach you can put into action
- remain optimistic and engage with the poem so that you are open to its feelings and ideas
- remember that there are time limits, so don't spend too long on note-making. Leave enough time to write your answer.

READING THE QUESTION

Decide what the key words are in the question and highlight these. For example:

'How does the **poet present** the **speaker's feelings** about **friendship**?'

So, write about:

- how the poet presents feelings and ideas about friendship (e.g. what vocabulary choices and techniques are chosen and their effects)
- how the speaker's voice portrays these feelings and ideas about friendship.

Keep the key words in mind as you write, or refer back to them so you stay on track.

For help writing annotations, see page 17.

For help using quotations, see page 19.

For how to approach Question 2, see page 29.

TOP TIP ★

Question 1, the question on the first poem, will gain you the most marks (**24**) so spend **about 30–35** minutes on this. Use the remaining time to answer Question 2, the question on both poems (**8 marks**).

HOW TO APPROACH QUESTION 1

You might find it useful to memorise the following stages so that when you answer the question you have a coherent approach to help you.

Stage 1
- Read the poem through and respond to it simply.
- Read the exam question and highlight the key words.

Stage 2
- Read the poem again, keeping the exam question in mind.
- Highlight important images and techniques that help you answer the question.

Stage 3
- Add some annotations to the poem.
- Reread any lines or images that you are unsure of, thinking about the broad meaning of the poem.

Stage 4
- Use your annotations to help you write your response.

GUIDE TO POETIC TECHNIQUES

In this section you are going to learn about the various poetic techniques that you will be identifying in the 'unseen' poems. You will then learn how to annotate a poem (page 17) and then read a variety of poems, each with a different focus (pages 18–27).

In order to answer the exam questions on the unseen poems, you will need to be able to recognise the **poetic techniques** described on the following pages. It is important, however, always to describe the **effect** a technique creates rather than just identifying it. Also remember that many techniques, such as rhythm and rhyme, or assonance and alliteration, work together to create or reinforce effects, usually of particular images and themes in a poem. Examples are given from the poems in this book and also from the AQA Anthology.

VOICE AND PERSPECTIVE

Voice/speaker

The voice, or speaker, is the person behind the words of the poem. The distinctive tone and style of the voice enables the reader to get to know the speaker. The speaker is the not the same as the poet.

Example	The speaker in the poem 'Salamander' (page 20) asks 'Does he think I am a salamander too?', making the assumption that the salamander thinks like a human, and might also view a human as a salamander.
Effect	The assumption in the question suggests a childlike innocence. In addition, the question underlines the need that the speaker has to make a friend of the salamander, reinforcing the speaker not only as a child, but a lonely one.

Perspective

The perspective is the point of view from which the poem is written and is usually third person or first person, past or present. Less often it is second person; this is when the speaker addresses another voice or the reader as 'you'.

Example	In 'Salamander' (page 20) the speaker recounts what is happening from the first person present perspective: 'I watch him'.
Effect	The first person present tense creates a sense of closeness as if the speaker is nearby.

Persona

If the **voice** in the poem is a specific person or character, rather like an actor playing a role, we refer to it as a **persona**.

Example	Dramatic monologues have personas. The speaker in Robert Browning's 'My Last Duchess' (AQA Anthology) is the Duke of Ferrara.
Effect	The effect is to create a dramatic voice, as though the character is centre stage, addressing an audience.

Mood

Mood is the tone or atmosphere created by the poet. Voice, vocabulary, rhythm and other techniques all combine to create the mood of the poem. Mood affects the reader's feelings.

Example	In Charlotte Mew's 'The Call' (page 40), the speaker asks 'Was it a bright or a dark angel? Who can know? / It left no mark upon the snow'.
Effect	A sense of mystery has been building from line 7 in the poem and reaches a height in these lines. The 'bright' or 'dark angel' creates a supernatural mood, but the use of questions makes the meaning **ambiguous**.

Colloquialism

Everyday language, which may include regional expressions or slang, is described as **colloquial**.

Example	In John Pownall's 'Moving' (page 60) the speaker refers to a woman's 'kids' instead of 'children'.
Effect	The effect is to help create a sense of the commonplace, so that the reader feels that the events and feelings in the poem, however important, are also part of an ordinary life.

FORM AND STRUCTURE   (A02)

Form

Form is the way the poem is laid out on the page. It can refer to a specific verse form in which the number of lines in a verse or **stanza** is repeated. It can also refer to a specific type of poem that follows a set of rules such as those for a **sonnet**. If a poem has no regular form it is usually called **free verse**. A poem's form often enhances its meaning.

Example	'Drummer Hodge' (page 36) has three sestets. It has repeated stanza lengths, line lengths and a regular metre.
Effect	The effect of the repetition creates formality, showing respect for Hodge. The stanzas create a simple funeral song (dirge).

Structure

Structure is the pattern, order or organisation of language and ideas and how they develop and change throughout the poem.

Example	In Lord Byron's 'When We Two Parted' (AQA Anthology), the speaker returns to the beginning of the poem at the end, so the poem is circular in structure. The key words 'In silence and tears' are repeated.
Effect	The effect of the circular structure is to convince the reader not only of the depth of the speaker's feelings about lost love, but also that the speaker is not free from the emotions expressed at the beginning of the poem, even 'After long years'.

Enjambment

Enjambment occurs when a line runs on into the next line without pause, carrying the thought, image, pace and sometimes the sound with it.

Example	In Paul Deaton's 'Sea Bream Dinner' (page 24) enjambment is used in the lines 'over the long broken / path'.
Effect	The first line flows into the second, taking the image of the 'path' with it. Since it also lengthens the line, it emphasises that the path is a 'long' one.

Caesura

Caesura is a pause in a line of poetry that affects the pace and rhythm.

Example	Caesura is used in Paul Deaton's 'Sea Bream Dinner' (page 24), in the lines 'be wholesome, silver sea thing, / treasured, let the white meat do its best.'
Effect	The pauses after 'wholesome' and 'treasured' help to create a slow, gentle pace. They emphasise the careful ritual involved in cooking the meal, while simultaneously showing respect for the fish that provides the nourishment.

Stanza

A **stanza** is a specific group of lines forming a unit, such as a **quatrain**. (A verse can be any number of lines that are grouped together and does not necessarily follow any specific pattern.)

Example	In Mike Gould's 'Installations' (page 22), for example, each stanza is made up of two lines – a **couplet**.
Effect	Individual couplets have been chosen to create the effect of separate images, reinforcing the idea that they are like pictures in a gallery.

Metre

Metre is the pattern of stressed and unstressed syllables in a line of verse. The most common metre in English is **iambic pentameter**.

Example	In Thomas Hardy's 'Drummer Hodge' (page 36) the line, 'They **throw** in **Drum**mer **Hodge**, to **rest**' is **iambic tetrameter** followed by the line 'Uncoffined – **just** as found', which is **iambic trimeter**. Line 1 begins with an unstressed syllable followed by a stressed syllable for four feet, and line 2 for three feet. (A foot is the different stress pattern in a unit of rhythm). The metre is kept up throughout the poem.
Effect	The heavy sound of the stressed syllables echo the heavy sound of soldiers marching or perhaps the powerful, repetitive movement of earth being shovelled into Hodges' grave.

Half-rhyme

A rhyme is a **half-rhyme** if it has the same consonants but not the same vowel sound. Half-rhyme is sometimes called 'slant-rhyme' or 'near-rhyme'.

Example	Half-rhyme occurs in Thomas Hardy's 'Neutral Tones' (AQA Anthology) as 'rove' and 'love'.
Effect	Half-rhyme is often used if the poet wishes to introduce a discordant note. Here, Hardy is writing about a broken relationship. The reader is therefore reminded of the **theme** through the choice of half-rhyme 'rove'/'love' (an imperfect rhyme, like the relationship).

LANGUAGE

Imagery

An **image** is a picture in words that makes objects, living things or actions feel more vivid in the reader's mind. It often appeals to the sense of sight, but may appeal to the other senses too.

Example	In Mike Gould's 'Installations' (page 22) there is an image of a dead fox's ribcage: 'a crimson diagram on tarmac plinth'.
Effect	The image has a dual effect. It reminds the reader of the gruesome and bloody nature of the fox's death. It also reminds us of a bright red painting or work of art set on a 'plinth', which is less immediate than the first effect.

Metaphor

A **metaphor** is a particular kind of image. It occurs when one thing is used to describe another, creating a striking impression.

Example	In Rupert Brooke's 'The Soldier' (page 37) the speaker-soldier says that whatever foreign field he might be buried in will become 'a richer dust'.
Effect	The speaker is saying that if the foreign field contains his body (an English body), it will be forever enriched. 'A richer dust' is a metaphor for English soil and therefore a patriotic metaphor for England.

Extended metaphor

An **extended metaphor** continues some aspect of the image. It may continue into the next line or throughout the poem.

Example	In, Carole Satyamurti's 'Piccadilly Line' (page 45) a comparison is made, throughout the whole poem, between a group of young girls and a moth (which dies). For example, the girls 'flutter', 'are excited by a vision / of glitter' and drawn 'to the lure of the light'.
Effect	The extended metaphor of the moth, its attraction to light and its brief life, gives the comparison greater weight, suggesting that youth is a very brief, if intense period of life.

Simile

A **simile** occurs when one thing is compared to another using 'like' or 'as'.

Example	Thomas Hardy's 'Neutral Tones' (AQA Anthology) includes the simile, 'And a grin of bitterness swept thereby / Like an ominous bird a-wing …' .
Effect	The speaker compares his companion's bitter smile to a sinister bird. The poet, therefore, drives home to the reader the complete failure of the relationship.

Connotation

Connotations are ideas that spring to mind or are suggested by a word or phrase.

Example	In Carole Satyamurti's 'Piccadilly Line' (page 45) the excited young girls who board the train on the underground line 'flutter' in their excitement at being out for the evening, then 'settle' down.
Effect	The verb 'flutter' has connotations of something light and insubstantial, such as a winged creature. However, when accompanied by the word 'settle', it suggests a moth in the specific circumstances of the poem.

Personification

Personification occurs when ideas or things are given human feelings and characteristics.

Example	In Percy Bysshe Shelley's 'Love's Philosophy' (AQA Anthology) 'the waves clasp one another'.
Effect	The reader sees in their mind's eye the natural movement of the waves holding each other in the way that a human might hug another human being.

Alliteration

Alliteration is the repetition of the same sound (not necessarily the same letter) in a stretch of language, often at the beginning of words.

Example	In Mike Gould's 'Installations' (page 22), 'digger's door' is alliterative.
Effect	The sound of double 'd' in **'digger's and door'** creates a heavy thudding sound that emphasises the bulk and weight of the bulldozer's cabin door.

Assonance

Assonance is the repetition of the same vowel sound in a stretch of language.

Example	Percy Bysshe Shelley's 'Love's Philosophy' (AQA Anthology) opens with the lines: 'The fountains mingle with the river / And the rivers with the Ocean / The winds of Heaven mix for ever / With a sweet emotion;'.
Effect	The repetition of the 'i' sound (in 'mingle', 'river', 'rivers', 'winds', mix, 'with') combines with the images of nature to reinforce the flowing movement of the river and wind.

Consonance

Consonance is the repetition of the same consonant sound in a stretch of language. (It is different from alliteration because, unlike alliteration, it concerns consonant sounds only.)

Example	In Elizabeth Barrett Browning's 'Sonnet 29 – I think of thee!' (AQA Anthology), 'straggling green', which is describing wild vines, is an example of consonance.
Effect	The repetition of 'g' in 'straggling' and 'green' helps to emphasise the image of the wayward, invasive vines.

Ambiguity

Ambiguity occurs when writers, perhaps deliberately, use words or images with more than one meaning or interpretation.

Example	In Charlotte Mew's 'The Call' (page 40) there is a visitor to the speaker's home: 'Something swift and tall / Swept in and out and that was all.'
Effect	The visitor that calls may be some kind of supernatural presence or a figment of the speaker's mind. The poet chooses to give the reader little certainty about what the presence is, in order to create a sense of mystery or a spiritual element to the narrator's experience.

Sibilant

The **sibilant** is a hissing sound made by using 's', 'ss' 'sh' or 'z'.

Example	In Charlotte Mew's 'The Farmer's Bride' (AQA Anthology), the young wife is described as, 'Shy as a leveret, swift as he / Straight and slight as a young larch tree'.
Effect	The soft sounding sibilant 's' in the repeated 'as', 'Shy', 'swift', 'Straight' and 'slight' and its association with the 'Shy ... leveret' and the 'young ... tree' helps reinforce in the reader's mind the darting but timid youthfulness and vulnerability of the young wife.

Rhetorical question

A **rhetorical question** is asked for effect; to persuade or further an argument rather than elicit an answer.

Example	The speaker in Percy Bysshe Shelley's 'Love's Philosophy' (AQA Anthology) asks at the end of the poem: 'And the sunlight clasps the earth, / And the moonbeams kiss the sea – / What are all these kissings worth, / If thou kiss not me?'
Effect	The question is used to further the argument that the lover should unite with the speaker, as the moon and sea unite.

HOW TO ANNOTATE A POEM

When you annotate a poem you scribble quick comments, questions and ideas around it, and sometimes on it, using circles, underlining or highlighting to help you focus.

ELEMENTS YOU MIGHT ANNOTATE

The poem's 'story'

Does the poem seem to be about something specific, such as a relationship or an incident? Sometimes a poem may seem to concentrate on feelings and thoughts rather than describe particular events. But a poem will always have a focus, and be about the speaker's experience.

Theme

What is the main idea or ideas running through the poem? If key lines reveal this, you could highlight them. Are there other related ideas you could also select? Remember, the theme or message is revealed through the 'story'.

Voice and perspective

Can you note down the mood the voice creates? Is it sad, thoughtful, distant? What person is the poem told in and what tense? Who is the speaker addressing?

Form

Is the poem written in a specific form, such as a sonnet? Is it free verse? Can you highlight any patterns? Although the line lengths vary in free verse, there may be repetition or rhymes that are not immediately obvious, which appear in the middle of sentences, for example. Rhythm, regular or irregular, and rhyme, such as in a rhyming couplet, give form to a poem.

Structure

How does the poem open and close? Does it change direction? Regular rhythm and rhyme can also be part of the structure and bring a sense of closure or finality, for example. You could make notes alongside the start and end of the poem.

Language

How does the poet use language? How does it link to the theme? What particular vocabulary choices and images can you highlight which the poet has used to create effects?

Poetic techniques

Can you identify any specific techniques? What effects are created? Remember that poetic techniques work together. For example, the vowels in assonance create sound effects that may, for example, highlight the mood.

The annotations below highlight some examples of the poem's elements. There are other examples too, so read the annotations and see what else you can find.

Use this process with all the poems you study.

Story: speaker is trying to reach a lover by text message, but there is a breakdown in the relationship and/or communication - main theme of the poem?

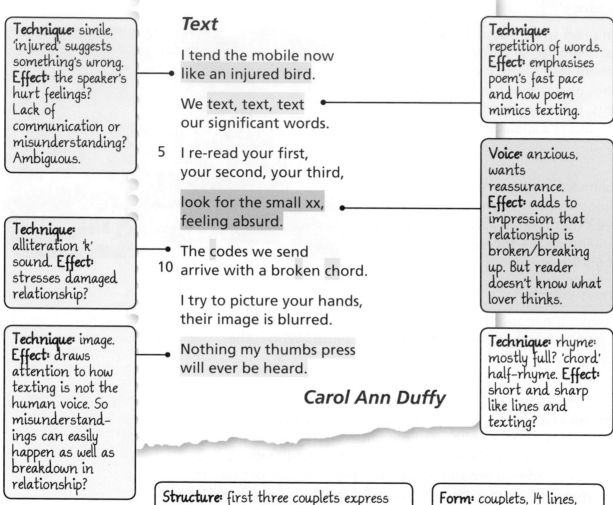

Technique: simile, 'injured' suggests something's wrong. **Effect:** the speaker's hurt feelings? Lack of communication or misunderstanding? Ambiguous.

Technique: alliteration 'k' sound. **Effect:** stresses damaged relationship?

Technique: image. **Effect:** draws attention to how texting is not the human voice. So misunderstandings can easily happen as well as breakdown in relationship?

Text

I tend the mobile now
like an injured bird.

We text, text, text
our significant words.

5   I re-read your first,
your second, your third,

look for the small xx,
feeling absurd.

The codes we send
10 arrive with a broken chord.

I try to picture your hands,
their image is blurred.

Nothing my thumbs press
will ever be heard.

Carol Ann Duffy

Technique: repetition of words. **Effect:** emphasises poem's fast pace and how poem mimics texting.

Voice: anxious, wants reassurance. **Effect:** adds to impression that relationship is broken/breaking up. But reader doesn't know what lover thinks.

Technique: rhyme: mostly full? 'chord' half-rhyme. **Effect:** short and sharp like lines and texting?

Structure: first three couplets express anxiety, fourth also includes feelings of foolishness. Last three - speaker thinks relationship is broken. Last one very final.

Form: couplets, 14 lines, a loose sonnet about love. Spaces between couplets suggest distance between lovers.

HOW TO USE QUOTATIONS

One of the secrets of success in writing exam essays is to use quotations *effectively*. There are five basic principles:

1 Only quote what is most useful.

2 Do not use a quotation that repeats what you have just written.

3 Put quotation marks around the quotation.

4 Write the quotation exactly as it appears in the original.

5 Use the quotation so that it fits neatly (is embedded) into your sentence.

Quotations should be used to develop the line of thought in your essay, and to 'zoom in' on key details, such as language choices. Compare the Good Level and High Level responses to 'The Letter' (page 53) below and the ways in which the quotations are used.

TOP TIP

Don't forget that you can quote several single words from a poem to explain a particular tone or idea; for example in exploring the 'semantic field' or in picking up patterns, repetitions or contrasts.

Good Level use of quotation: **clear** and **logical**

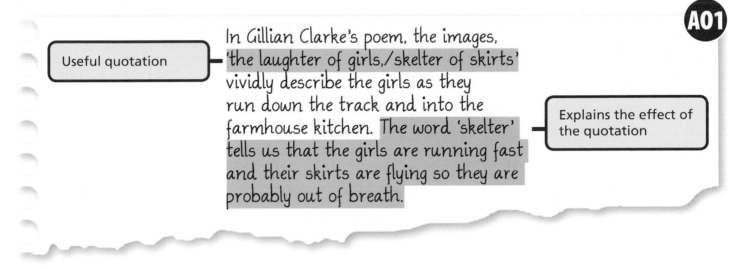

A01

Useful quotation

In Gillian Clarke's poem, the images, 'the laughter of girls,/skelter of skirts' vividly describe the girls as they run down the track and into the farmhouse kitchen. The word 'skelter' tells us that the girls are running fast and their skirts are flying so they are probably out of breath.

Explains the effect of the quotation

High Level use of quotation: **precise focus** with comment on **connotations and effects**

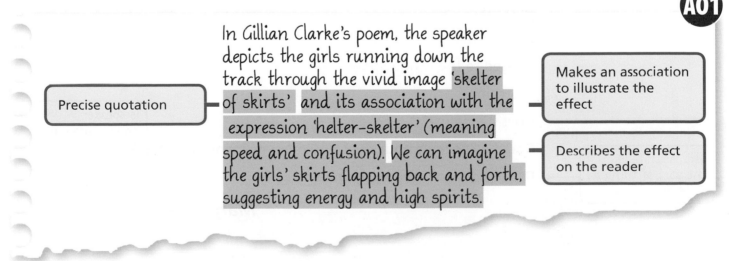

A01

In Gillian Clarke's poem, the speaker depicts the girls running down the track through the vivid image 'skelter of skirts' and its association with the expression 'helter-skelter' (meaning speed and confusion). We can imagine the girls' skirts flapping back and forth, suggesting energy and high spirits.

Precise quotation

Makes an association to illustrate the effect

Describes the effect on the reader

VOICE AND PERSPECTIVE

Start by reading the following poem, which explores ideas about loneliness and friendship. The student's annotations in this case relate to **voice** and **perspective** and how these contribute to the poem's effects.

Salamander

An unexpected guest

Comes to my grandmother's greenhouse,

> Could be a child speaking?

A golden salamander,

Searching for slugs,

> Speaker is looking for friendship

5 And company, perhaps.

On lonely days I watch him.

> Voice is sad/ resigned

> Present tense rather than past tense. Effect?

He is a clown tumbling between chrysanthemums

And red geraniums,

> A word a child might use

Or a shadow puppet

> Quite difficult word for a child

10 Darting between shady leaves

And the roots of miniature trees.

Or sometimes he lolls

In the luxury of the African marigold,

As though sunning himself in its glow.

> First person speaker. Effect?

15 I am as still as a waxwork.

He spots my presence

And sits,

His eyes mapping my face

Pressed to the windowpane.

20 Searching.

Does he see me?

Does he know we both wear the colour of friendship?

> Is speaker addressing him/ herself or reader — or who?

> This sounds like the sort of thing a child would say.

Does he think I am a salamander too?

Mary Green

WORKING FROM THE ANNOTATIONS

Through exploring the **voice** you can find out about the speaker of the poem, where they are, what they are thinking and feeling, and sometimes who they are. The annotations on **perspective** tell us what person and tense the poem is written in. Both can add to our understanding of the poem and its mood.

1 What have you discovered about the poem from the annotations? What could you add? Write further comments alongside the poem. For example:

● Find any other lines or words that suggest whether the speaker is an adult or a child (e.g. in lines 7–14).

● Try to answer any questions asked in the annotations.

2 What do the annotations tell you about the speaker's voice and perspective and the effects these create? Think about:

● how the speaker's voice shifts in tone in the last lines of the poem and the effect this has on the reader.

TOP TIP

Remember, the speaker is not the poet. The speaker of the poem is the voice that you imagine when you read a poem. While a poet may draw on their experience, the poem is not an autobiography. Even very personal poems are always works of imagination.

EXAM FOCUS   **A01** **A02**

A student has begun to write about the voice in the poem and the nature of the speaker and how it reflects loneliness and a search for friendship.

> Reference to voice

> Considers more than one possibility about who the speaker could be

The speaker of the poem seems to be a 'lonely' child. The poem employs complex words, such as 'chrysanthemum' in line 7, which a child might not use, but the last line sounds very like a child who is imagining how the salamander thinks. It is as if the speaker feels the salamander and he or she might have a connection and be real friends.

> Identifies how the speaker feels and embeds quotation in sentence

> Shows the effect on the reader

YOUR TASK

3 Write at least two paragraphs, similar in style to the one above, discussing other features of the voice and perspective. Remember to include evidence and refer back to your answers to Questions 1 and 2. You could write about the following:

● The perspective (person and tense) of the poem and the effects created.

● How the voice changes in mood and its effects. (Refer here to your answer in Question 2.)

● How the speaker's mood is reflected in particular words. For example, consider the importance of the word 'Searching' in the last verse. Is it only the salamander that is 'searching'?

● Anything else you can think of.

FORM AND STRUCTURE

You are now going to look at a student's annotations on the uses of **form** and **structure**, in a poem which explores ideas about art and the way we see reality. As you read the poem, consider how structural elements contribute to its effects.

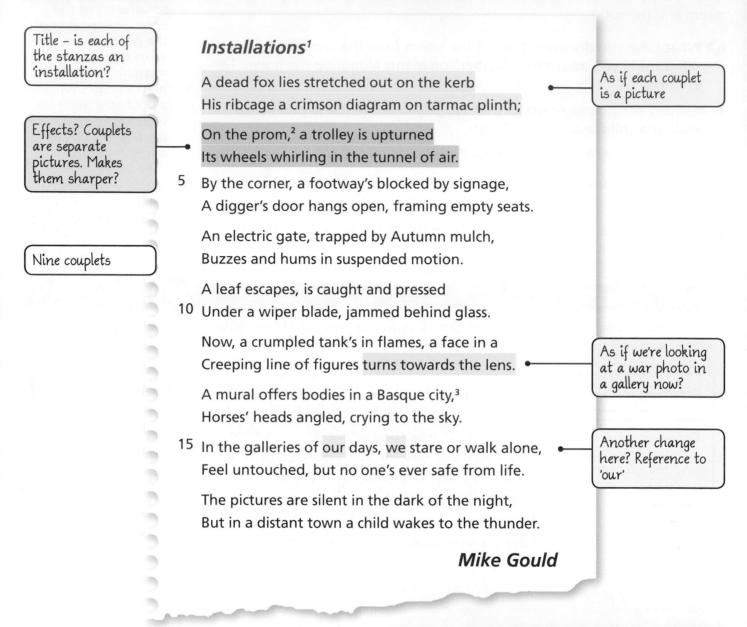

> Title – is each of the stanzas an 'installation'?

> Effects? Couplets are separate pictures. Makes them sharper?

> Nine couplets

> As if each couplet is a picture

> As if we're looking at a war photo in a gallery now?

> Another change here? Reference to 'our'

Installations[1]

A dead fox lies stretched out on the kerb
His ribcage a crimson diagram on tarmac plinth;

On the prom,[2] a trolley is upturned
Its wheels whirling in the tunnel of air.

5 By the corner, a footway's blocked by signage,
A digger's door hangs open, framing empty seats.

An electric gate, trapped by Autumn mulch,
Buzzes and hums in suspended motion.

A leaf escapes, is caught and pressed
10 Under a wiper blade, jammed behind glass.

Now, a crumpled tank's in flames, a face in a
Creeping line of figures turns towards the lens.

A mural offers bodies in a Basque city,[3]
Horses' heads angled, crying to the sky.

15 In the galleries of our days, we stare or walk alone,
Feel untouched, but no one's ever safe from life.

The pictures are silent in the dark of the night,
But in a distant town a child wakes to the thunder.

Mike Gould

Glossary

1 'Installations' are modern works of art, often with several different parts to them, and are usually exhibited in a gallery space.

   'Installation' can also refer to something installed or put into a space or room.

2 promenade; a path, usually along a seafront

3 Reference to Picasso's painting 'Guernica' about a city bombed during the Spanish Civil War (1936–9)

WORKING FROM THE ANNOTATIONS

Form and **structure** are both important because they help signal changes in direction, or direct the reader towards particular ideas, sounds or patterns. The way a poem is divided up can also isolate particular ideas or images, so that they create impact and meaning.

1 What have you discovered about the poem from the annotations? Is there anything else you could add about the structure? Write further comments alongside the poem. You might think about whether any words or sounds are repeated or echoed, even if rhyme is not used.

2 What have you learned from the annotations about the structure and how it contributes to the poem's effect? Think about how it affects the:

- meaning of the poem and how it helps the poet express himself
- way the reader feels or thinks about the poem.

> **TOP TIP** ⭐
>
> Remember, as a rough guide, the **form** is the way the poem is laid out and sometimes has a name, such as 'free verse'. The **structure** is the underlying pattern and direction the poem takes.

EXAM FOCUS **A01** **A02** ✏️

A student has begun a response, referring to the way the poem reflects the idea of art through its structure.

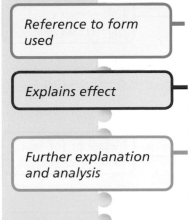

Reference to form used ——
Explains effect ——

— **Close reading of stanza**
— **Chooses appropriate quotations**

Further explanation and analysis

The writer has divided the poem into nine separate couplets. In each one of these, except the seventh, it is as if the poet has hung up an image for us to look at, like the 'dead fox' in the first and the trolley in the second. Because these images are separated like this, they are very clear – as though they are framed in a gallery. This initially creates a sense of distance, even coldness.

YOUR TASK

3 Write at least two paragraphs, similar in style to the one above, on other aspects of the form or structure of the poem. You could choose to write about some or all of the following:

- How each of the first five couplets reflect everyday life – and the tone/mood created.
- The change in focus in the sixth stanza.
- Why the eighth stanza refers to 'our' and 'we' and the change in mood this creates.
- Anything else you can think of.

LANGUAGE

When you explore a poem's language, think about how it reveals the ideas and **themes** in the poem. Read 'Sea Bream Dinner', which explores ideas about nourishment, mealtime rituals and respect for food.

The student's annotations highlight features of the language and how these contribute to the poem's effects.

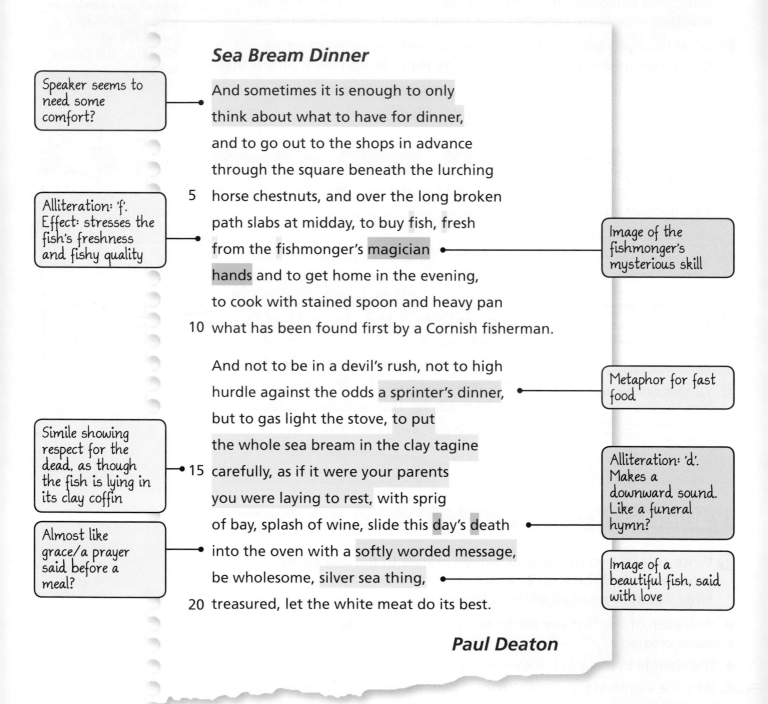

Sea Bream Dinner

Speaker seems to need some comfort?

And sometimes it is enough to only

think about what to have for dinner,

and to go out to the shops in advance

through the square beneath the lurching

5　horse chestnuts, and over the long broken

path slabs at midday, to buy fish, fresh

Alliteration: 'f'. Effect: stresses the fish's freshness and fishy quality

from the fishmonger's magician

Image of the fishmonger's mysterious skill

hands and to get home in the evening,

to cook with stained spoon and heavy pan

10　what has been found first by a Cornish fisherman.

And not to be in a devil's rush, not to high

hurdle against the odds a sprinter's dinner,

Metaphor for fast food

but to gas light the stove, to put

the whole sea bream in the clay tagine

Simile showing respect for the dead, as though the fish is lying in its clay coffin

15　carefully, as if it were your parents

you were laying to rest, with sprig

of bay, splash of wine, slide this day's death

Alliteration: 'd'. Makes a downward sound. Like a funeral hymn?

Almost like grace/a prayer said before a meal?

into the oven with a softly worded message,

be wholesome, silver sea thing,

Image of a beautiful fish, said with love

20　treasured, let the white meat do its best.

Paul Deaton

WORKING FROM THE ANNOTATIONS

Poetic language appeals to our feelings and senses and is used in many different ways to create effects. It includes a wide range of techniques, the most common of which is the image.

TOP TIP

Remember that a single poem can include different kinds of language, such as everyday expressions and unusual images.

1 What have you discovered about the poem from the annotations? What could you add? Write further comments about the language choices alongside the poem. For example, think about lines 3–6 and how the speaker feels about his situation and urban environment. What do 'long broken / path slabs' suggest?

2 Look for further examples of alliteration in the first verse (such as the sibilant in lines 6–8). What do they remind you of? What effect do they create?

EXAM FOCUS   **A01** **A02**

A student has begun a response focusing on the speaker's attitude to the fish through the language chosen.

Good choice of vocabulary to describe the preparing of the fish

The poem describes the preparation of sea bream for a meal. Preparing the fish is like a sacred ritual. The 'clay tagine' in which the fish is laid is its coffin and the simile 'as if it were your parents / you were laying to rest' reminds us of a funeral service and respect for the dead. The overall effect of these images is to remind us not only how important food is, but also that we should show respect for the creatures we eat.

Topic sentence outlines the poem's story

Identifies the images and their effects on the reader

Develops explanation to show the wider effect of the images

YOUR TASK

3 Write at least two paragraphs, similar in style to the one above on aspects of the language. Remember to include evidence and refer back to your answers in Questions 1 and 2. You could choose to write about some or all of the following:

● How the poem opens, and what it tells you about how the speaker feels about preparing a good meal.

● The vivid images of the fish created by different examples of alliteration in lines 6–8.

● What the speaker's usual working day and eating habits are like. (Look at the colloquial language and vocabulary choices used at the beginning of the second verse.)

● Anything else you can think of.

WORKED TASK

Read the following poem and annotation, and the question that
follows, which is similar to a question 1 from Section C: Unseen poetry.

Green Thought

I do not know much about love, but I know

It is common as grass which, although

It refuse at times to take root on a lawn,

Can bury a bombsite, split asphalt,[1] and grow

5   In any ditch, niche, or gutter where winds blow

Or sparrow-boys brawl. This much I learn

From an old man who has limped up the path

To warm his feet, and more than his feet, at our hearth.

His scrupulous tweeds and courtesy

10 Have taken their place in the ritual tea

On Sunday afternoons: a ritual

For him, whose shrine this is, especially.

A girl, not yet his wife, runs for more tea

Into the singing kitchen. From the hall

15 Her footsteps chatter, and soon her face

Will laugh in the mirror over the mantlepiece.

He is watching – over his cup, between

Fireplace and door – a princess not nineteen.

We too remember her: though she appears

20 To us as the tall, gaunt, tragedy-queen

Whom illness kept indoors, who dressed in green

Throughout all seasons. We remember tears;

Agonies the doctors could not understand;

Tantrums, and the last tantrum ended by her hand.

> Reference to the 'girl' is in the past

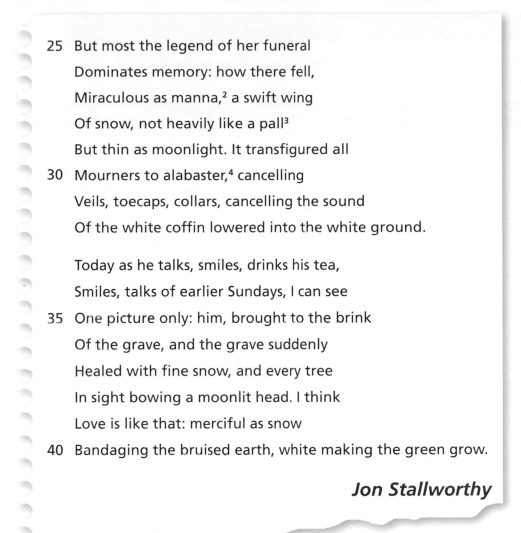

25 But most the legend of her funeral

Dominates memory: how there fell,

Miraculous as manna,² a swift wing

Of snow, not heavily like a pall³

But thin as moonlight. It transfigured all

30 Mourners to alabaster,⁴ cancelling

Veils, toecaps, collars, cancelling the sound

Of the white coffin lowered into the white ground.

Today as he talks, smiles, drinks his tea,

Smiles, talks of earlier Sundays, I can see

35 One picture only: him, brought to the brink

Of the grave, and the grave suddenly

Healed with fine snow, and every tree

In sight bowing a moonlit head. I think

Love is like that: merciful as snow

40 Bandaging the bruised earth, white making the green grow.

Jon Stallworthy

Glossary

¹ a dark substance used for surfacing roads

² food from heaven (in the Bible)

³ a cloth spread over a coffin; a thick, dark cloud of smoke

⁴ almost transparent, white stone

QUESTION

In 'Green Thought' how does the poet present the speaker's feelings about love and loss?

WHAT TO LOOK FOR

The question suggests that you will need to look for particular features to answer the question well. For example:

- what is happening and has happened in the poem
- attitudes to love and what love means to the speaker and the visitor
- how you think the events have affected the speaker's feelings about love, death and nature
- the language, form and voice the poet has chosen. (Remember you will need to look for evidence and techniques used and discuss their effects.)

❶ Keeping the question and bullet points in mind, add your own annotations to the poem.

TOP TIP ⭐

Most poems have some kind of 'story'. They describe the speaker's thoughts and may include events, if only a few. This is not the same as a 'narrative' poem, which has a storyline of some length. Ballads are traditional examples of narrative poems.

WRITING YOUR ANSWER

You can structure your answer in different ways. Here is one possible approach:

Paragraph	Main points	Example/evidence
Introduction	Outline briefly the story's poem in one or two sentences. You can also add a comment about what you think the poet is presenting.	*The speaker in 'Green Thought' describes the visit of an elderly man. He imagines the visitor's deep feelings and recalls the memories surrounding the death of the visitor's wife 'by her hand'. Through these events, the poet presents ideas about love and loss.*
Paragraphs 2–4	You could write about the speaker's thoughts on love (stanza 1), and what he imagines the elderly man's thoughts are (stanzas 2 and 3).	
Paragraphs 5–6	Discuss why the funeral is particularly important and how this affects the speaker's attitude to love and death. Mention the importance of nature and what it represents (stanzas 4 and 5).	
Conclusion	Sum up concisely the feelings and ideas the poet is presenting to the reader. (Do not discuss all the main points again.)	

② Using the plan above (or a plan of your own) write an answer to the question.

PROGRESS CHECK

GOOD PROGRESS

I can:

- understand voice and perspective in an unseen poem and describe its effects. ☐
- understand form and structure in an unseen poem and describe it effects. ☐
- identify several examples of the way language is used and describe their effects. ☐

EXCELLENT PROGRESS

I can:

- analyse voice and perspective and how it may change in an unseen poem. ☐
- analyse form and structure in an unseen poem and describe its effects. ☐
- analyse a wide range of language in an unseen poem and describe its various effects. ☐

PART THREE: COMPARING 'UNSEEN' POEMS

QUESTION 2 – COMPARING THE POEMS

In Paper 2, Section C: Unseen poetry, Question 2 will ask you to identify the similarities and differences between the poem you have written about in Question 1 and another unseen poem.

READING THE QUESTION

A typical question might focus on how the:

- speaker of the poem describes feelings
- poet presents these feelings.

For example:

Question 2: In both 'Poem for My Sister' and 'To a Daughter Leaving Home' the speakers describe feelings about watching someone they love grow up. What are the similarities and/or differences between the ways the poets present these feelings?

ANNOTATING THE SECOND POEM

For Question 2, you will be juggling two poems and their different sets of ideas and features. You therefore need to have a coherent approach that you can trust in the exam and that enables you to answer the question clearly and quickly. For example:

- Read the second poem through quickly to gain a quick understanding of its story.
- Annotate the second poem only, noting similarities (S) and differences (D) between the two poems.
- Highlight or underline key quotations. Don't write them down – it takes too long.
- Note any poetic techniques you recognise that help you answer the question, highlighting or underlining the relevant words.

> **TOP TIP** ⭐
>
> Remember you will only have time to write about **three or four paragraphs** for Question 2.

WRITING YOUR RESPONSE

Since the second question has fewer marks (8) than the first (24), **compare** only the poems' **most important similarities** and **differences**. You will not have time to mention everything you notice but make sure above all else that you demonstrate close analysis of the language, form and structure, and voice and perspective, and their effect.

There are different approaches here, too:

- One approach is to write a couple of paragraphs about the similarities between the poems, then follow with paragraphs about the differences.
- A second, more fluent approach that could gain you more marks is to compare and contrast points *within a paragraph* before you move on to a new paragraph. To avoid contradicting yourself, use connectives such as 'however' or 'in the same way'.

COMPARING AND LANGUAGE FEATURES

When exploring the language in both poems only focus on what seems to be significant.

- Do the poems use similar images about love, nature or whatever the theme happens to be?

- Are the images different? Perhaps some are similar and others are different?

Read how a student has compared two poems, commenting on **similarities** and **differences** in the way the language depicts two young girls in 'Sally' (page 62) and 'Green Thought' (page 26). Key structure and contrast words have been highlighted.

> Like Sally, in Phoebe Hesketh's poem, the early depiction of the young girl in Jon Stallworthy's 'Green Thought' is an optimistic one. The image of the girl running 'into the singing kitchen' suggests not only her voice, but also her youthful happiness, which affects the general mood in the kitchen. By contrast, while Sally retains her 'shine' at the end of Hesketh's poem, the young girl in 'Green Thought' becomes a troubled young woman.

COMPARING FORM AND STRUCTURE

When you compare and contrast the form and structure of the two poems, note any poetic forms you recognise and any particular features of structure. For example, can you see evidence of any common verse patterns, repetitions, pauses in a line (caesura) or a line that runs on into another (enjambment)? Also note any similar or contrasting patterns or changes in the way the poem evolves or tells its 'story'.

Read how a student has compared 'Installations' (page 22) and 'Text' (page 18), commenting on the **similarities** and **differences** in the form and structure. As before, key structure and contrast words have been highlighted.

> Both 'Installations' and 'Text' are written in couplets. The spaces in between the couplets create a particular effect in each poem. In the former, they help to make each image separate, mimicking pictures in a gallery. In the latter, the spaces suggest the gap that has opened up between the two lovers, for unlike 'Installations', 'Text' is also a sonnet. It is a loose, modern one of fourteen lines with love as its theme – a typical theme for a sonnet. In contrast, the theme in 'Installations' focuses on the difference between art and life.

COMPARING VOICE AND PERSPECTIVE

When you compare and contrast the voice and perspective in the two poems, consider the moods they help to create.

- Is the voice direct? Does it seem near or distant? For example, the use of the first person can create a 'close-up' effect.
- Does the voice in the other poem create a similar mood to the first or is it distant and reflective?
- Do the voices shift in mood?

Read how a student has compared two poems, commenting on **similarities** and **differences** in the voice and perspective of 'The Call' (page 40) and 'Piccadilly Line (page 45). As before, key structure and contrast words have been highlighted.

'The Call' is largely written in the first person plural past tense and yet the voice has a sense of immediacy. 'To-night we heard a call' grabs our attention and creates the feeling that the speaker is talking directly to us, rather like a storyteller might. A similar sense of immediacy is felt in 'Piccadilly Line' but through the use of the third person present tense. However, the mood evoked in the two poems is different. In 'Piccadilly Line' the 'chattering' voices of the excited young women are reflected in the quick, alert voice of the speaker who is watching them. In 'The Call' the voice has a sense of urgency and mystery. The speaker 'must arise and go' into an unknown 'dark' world.

Finally, remember that there are only **8 marks** available for this question, so focus on only the most powerful or important points of comparison or contrast.

KEY ADVICE: COMPARING UNSEEN POEMS

- Don't forget to write about similarities and differences.
- Refer back to the first poem when you make a point about the second.
- Include *short* quotations to support your points and embed them in a sentence.
- Make sure you understand any techniques (such as 'metaphor') that you recognise before commenting on them.
- Always describe the effects of any techniques you mention.

SIMILARITIES

Remember, you will have to answer a question on the first poem (24 marks) before you compare it with the second poem.

Here are the annotations a student has added to the first poem based on a question about the speaker's feelings about her mother.

Title: Magician's words before a trick

Form – free verse enjambment, no punctuation makes poem very easy to read?

Speaker respects mother's knowledge; is proud of her. Repeated for emphasis?

Structure shifts. Specific comic event described

Comic image of children like birds, curious chicks or ducklings?

Comic mood? Children watch (spellbound?) as mother performs the 'operation'?

Abra-Cadabra

My mother had more magic
in her thumb
than the length and breadth
of any magician

5   Weaving incredible stories
around the dark-green senna[1] brew
just to make us slake[2]
the ritual Sunday purgative

Knowing how to place a cochineal poultice
10   on a fevered forehead
Knowing how to measure a bully's symmetry
kneading the narah[3] pains away

Once my baby sister stuffed
a split-pea up her nostril
15   my mother got a crochet needle
and gently tried to pry it out

We stood around her
like inquisitive gauldings[4]

Suddenly, in surgeon's tone she ordered,
20   'Pass the black pepper,'
and patted a little
under the dozing nose

My baby sister sneezed.
The rest was history.

Grace Nichols

Speaker – adult looking back to childhood. Third person past tense helps to evoke the past

Enjambment

Mother – like a wise woman or witch? Making up stories like spells to persuade children to drink herbal remedy

Enjambment is used in six of the seven stanzas.

Mother's authority; commanding voice

Meaning the pea shot out, but also refers to the speaker's past? Strong memories?

Glossary

1   plant used to clear the bowel
2   quench
3   stomach
4   herons

Now read the second poem below so that you get a first impression of it. Quickly write down what you think it is about, its 'story', in a couple of sentences.

Lineage

My grandmothers were strong.

They followed plows and bent to toil.

They moved through fields sowing seed.

They touched earth and grain grew.

5   They were full of sturdiness and singing.

My grandmothers are full of memories

Smelling of soap and onions and wet clay

With veins rolling roughly over quick hands

They have many clean words to say.

10   My grandmothers were strong.

Why am I not as they?

Margaret Walker

Read the question below. The key words have been highlighted.

QUESTION

In **both poems**, 'Abra-Cadabra' and 'Lineage', the **speakers describe feelings** about **their mother or grandmothers**. What are the *similarities* between the ways the **poets present** these **feelings?**

Below are examples of a student's annotations on the second poem. Remember that these only highlight the *similarities* between 'Abra-Cadabra' and 'Lineage'.

❶ Look at the annotations on 'Lineage' below and add further annotations of your own to show how it is *similar* to 'Abra-Cadabra'.

Think about how:

- Margaret Walker presents the grandmothers' character traits and how this links to the way Grace Nichols presents the mother in 'Abra-Cadabra'
- the speaker describes the grandmothers' relationship to nature and how this is similar to the mother in 'Abra-Cadabra'
- Walker presents memory through a sense of family history and how this is depicted by Nichols.

> The title means family kinship, ancestors, reminding us of the importance of the mother in 'Abra-Cadabra'

> The appeal to smell and taste in both poems (e.g. 'senna brew' in 'Abra-Cadabra') helps to make the speaker's memories appear strong

Lineage

My grandmothers were strong.

They followed plows and bent to toil.

They moved through fields sowing seed.

They touched earth and grain grew.

5 They were full of sturdiness and singing.

My grandmothers are full of memories

Smelling of soap and onions and wet clay

With veins rolling roughly over quick hands

They have many clean words to say.

10 My grandmothers were strong.

Why am I not as they?

Margaret Walker

> The speakers in both poems have strong memories of their families

> The speaker is looking back at her grandmothers' lives. Compares with the speaker in 'Abra-Cadabra' who is looking back at childhood

EXAM FOCUS

(A01) (A02)

Here a student has begun a High Level answer using their annotations to comment on the similarities between 'Abra-Cadabra' and 'Lineage'.

Useful connective to introduce similarity

Quotation successfully embedded

In both poems the poet presents pictures of compelling female relations. In 'Lineage' the speaker's grandmothers were 'full of sturdiness' and 'followed plows and bent to toil', the nouns 'toil' and 'sturdiness' giving the reader a vivid image of hardy, robust women who worked on the land. In 'Abra-Cadabra' the poet creates an image of the mother's wisdom partly through her knowledge of herbal remedies, so that we see her as a commanding presence able to perform 'magic'.

Shows the effects on the reader of imagery

2 Using your annotations, write two more paragraphs on the similarities between the two poems.

To help improve your critical style, use a variety of verbs to describe effects. For example instead of saying 'The poet shows', or 'The poet tells us' you could use the following:

TOP TIP

Try using a selection of these verbs to write paragraphs on individual points about the poems in this book.

The poet ...	I/we/the ...
suggests	infer(s)
implies	recognise(s)
presents	reflect(s)
explores	understand(s)
demonstrates	question(s)
conveys	see(s)
describes	respond(s)

Here are some useful connectives that should help you to refer to similarities:

both	in the same way	also
as	likewise	similarly

DIFFERENCES

Remember, you will have to answer a question on the first poem (24 marks) before you compare it with the second poem.

Here are the annotations a student has added to the first poem based on a question about the speaker's feelings about war and death.

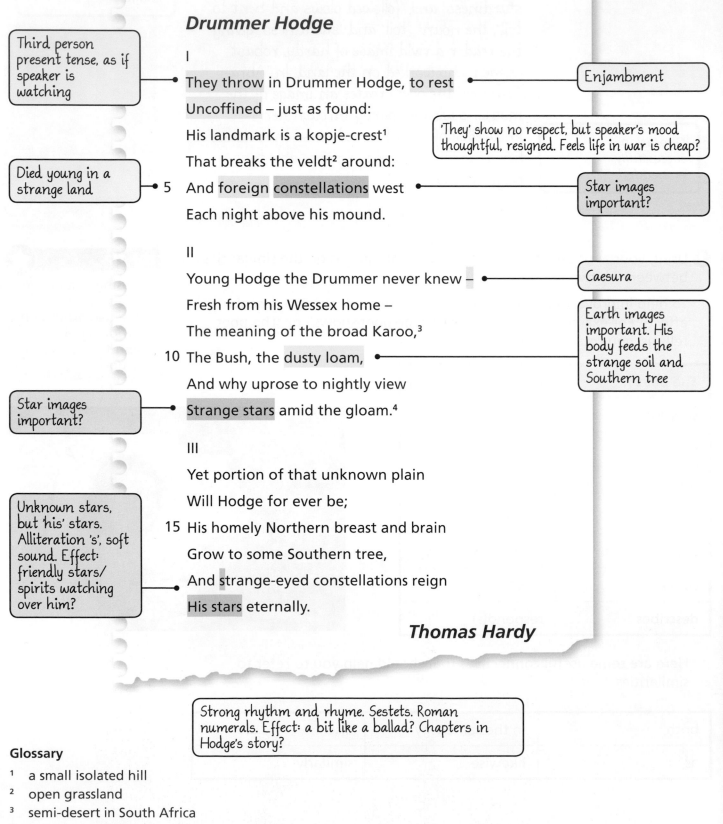

Drummer Hodge

Third person present tense, as if speaker is watching

I

They throw in Drummer Hodge, to rest — *Enjambment*

Uncoffined – just as found:

'They' show no respect, but speaker's mood thoughtful, resigned. Feels life in war is cheap?

His landmark is a kopje-crest[1]

Died young in a strange land

That breaks the veldt[2] around:

5 And foreign constellations west — *Star images important?*

Each night above his mound.

II

Young Hodge the Drummer never knew – — *Caesura*

Fresh from his Wessex home –

The meaning of the broad Karoo,[3]

Earth images important. His body feeds the strange soil and Southern tree

10 The Bush, the dusty loam, —

And why uprose to nightly view

Star images important?

Strange stars amid the gloam.[4]

III

Yet portion of that unknown plain

Will Hodge for ever be;

Unknown stars, but 'his' stars. Alliteration 's', soft sound. Effect: friendly stars/ spirits watching over him?

15 His homely Northern breast and brain

Grow to some Southern tree,

And strange-eyed constellations reign

His stars eternally.

Thomas Hardy

Strong rhythm and rhyme. Sestets. Roman numerals. Effect: a bit like a ballad? Chapters in Hodge's story?

Glossary

[1] a small isolated hill

[2] open grassland

[3] semi-desert in South Africa

[4] just after sunset

Now read the second poem below so that you get a first impression of it. Quickly write down what you think it is about, its 'story', in no more than a couple of sentences.

The Soldier

If I should die, think only this of me:
    That there's some corner of a foreign field
That is for ever England. There shall be
    In that rich earth a richer dust concealed;
5   A dust whom England bore, shaped, made aware,
    Gave, once, her flowers to love, her ways to roam,
A body of England's, breathing English air,
    Washed by the rivers, blest by the suns of home.

And think, this heart, all evil shed away,
10   A pulse in the eternal mind, no less
    Gives somewhere back the thoughts by England given;
Her sights and sounds; dreams happy as her day;
    And laughter, learnt of friends; and gentleness,
    In hearts at peace, under an English heaven.

Rupert Brooke

Read the question below. The key words have been highlighted.

QUESTION

In **both poems**, 'Drummer Hodge' and 'The Soldier' the **speakers describe feelings** about **war and death.** What are the *differences* between the ways the **poets present** these **feelings**?

Below are examples of a student's annotations on the second poem. Remember, they only highlight the *differences* between 'Drummer Hodge' and 'The Soldier'.

1 Look at the annotations on 'The Soldier' below and add further annotations of your own to show how it is *different* from 'Drummer Hodge'.

Think about:

● how the poet presents attitudes to war and how this differs from the way Hardy presents war in 'Drummer Hodge'

● how the speaker regards the 'foreign field' compared to the 'unknown plain' where Drummer Hodge lies

● the language Brooke uses to present England. (Clue: Look at the nature and religious imagery.) Contrast this with Hardy's depiction of the land.

The Soldier

First person

Speaker patriotic, values England, the land that 'made' him

Form – a sonnet. First stanza an octave, second a sestet. Poem is about 'love' – of country

If I should die, think only this of me:
　　That there's some corner of a foreign field
That is for ever England. There shall be
　　In that rich earth a richer dust concealed;
5　A dust whom England bore, shaped, made aware,
　　Gave, once, her flowers to love, her ways to roam,
A body of England's, breathing English air,
　　Washed by the rivers, blest by the suns of home.

And think, this heart, all evil shed away,
10　A pulse in the eternal mind, no less
　　Gives somewhere back the thoughts by England given;
Her sights and sounds; dreams happy as her day;
　　And laughter, learnt of friends; and gentleness,
　　In hearts at peace, under an English heaven.

Rupert Brooke

EXAM FOCUS

(A01) (A02)

Here a student has begun a Good Level answer using their annotations to comment on the differences between 'Drummer Hodge' and 'The Soldier'.

> Useful connective showing contrast

> Shows the effects of choice of form

In contrast to 'Drummer Hodge', in which life in war is presented as cheap, the speaker in 'The Soldier' emphasises patriotism. He believes that it is honourable to die for one's country; the country that has 'shaped' him. In addition, Brooke has chosen the sonnet, a form that celebrates love and reinforces one of the poem's main themes: love of one's country. Hardy, on the other hand, chooses a ballad-type tribute with a down-to-earth song-like quality that suits the story of an ordinary drummer boy killed in war.

> Identifies a main theme

> Quotation embedded in the sentence

> Contrasts the two forms

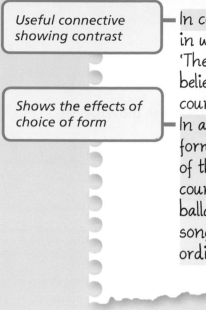

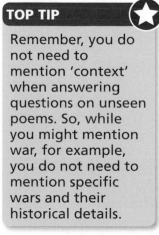

TOP TIP

When comparing unseen poems, remember that you need to decide what similarities and differences seem to be most important. For example, in 'The Soldier', mentioning the form – a sonnet – is a good idea since it links closely to one of the main themes, 'love', and contrasts with 'Drummer Hodge'.

❷ Using your annotations, write two paragraphs on the differences between the two poems.

Here are some useful connectives that should help you compare differences and illustrate and emphasise your points:

Contrasting	Illustrating	Emphasising
by contrast	for example	most of all
alternatively	for instance	in particular/ particularly
on the other hand	such as	especially
unlike	in this way	notably

TOP TIP

Remember, you do not need to mention 'context' when answering questions on unseen poems. So, while you might mention war, for example, you do not need to mention specific wars and their historical details.

WORKED TASK

Read the following poems and annotations and the question that follows,
which is similar to a Question 2 in Paper 2, Section C: Unseen poetry.

The Call

From our low seat beside the fire

Where we have dozed and dreamed and watched the glow

Or raked the ashes, stopping so

We scarcely saw the sun or rain

5   Above, or looked much higher

Than this same quiet red or burned-out fire.

To-night we heard a call,

A rattle on the window-pane,

A voice on the sharp air,

10   And felt a breath stirring our hair,

A flame within us: Something swift and tall

Swept in and out and that was all.

Was it a bright or dark angel? Who can know?

It left no mark upon the snow,

15   But suddenly it snapped the chain

Unbarred, flung wide the door

Which will not shut again;

And so we cannot sit here any more.

We must arise and go:

20   The world is cold without

And dark and hedged about

With mystery and enmity[1] and doubt,

But we must go

Though yet we do not know

25   Who called, or what marks we shall leave upon the snow.

Charlotte Mew

> Stark image of a strange voice calling, suggests danger or urgency.

Glossary

[1] hostility, ill-will

Canto[1] CCCLXIV

Occasionally, my sleeping baby girl

wakes alone within the darkened room,

lets out the saddest little drawn out wail

> Another image, this time of a sad wail, suggests human fears felt when asleep or in dreams.

then falls asleep again. The summer moon

5   glints icily through our uneven blinds,

a helicopter judders through the gloom

a dog across the road barks and then grinds

his canines against his new favourite stick.

There's never a moment when you cannot find

10   something that's crying out, but if you pick

a random living room, you'll find instead

a roaring soul within a nest of brick,

a trembling lip, a hairline bead of sweat,

a knot within the stomach, a slight tick,

15   a mental rerun of a great regret

that will not be alchemised[2] into talk,

nor find throat in primal,[3] mammalian[4] cries,

the expression rises within, then balks,[5]

returns to its cramped cell behind the eyes.

Niall O'Sullivan

Glossary

[1]   a 'canto' is the way a long poem is divided up; also means 'song' or 'singing'

[2]   altered by magic/early form of chemistry

[3]   relating to an early stage of development

[4]   of a mammal

[5]   hesitates

QUESTION

In both 'The Call' and 'Canto CCCLXIV' the speakers describe feelings about our inner thoughts and fears and how they might or might not be expressed. What are the similarities and/or differences between the ways the poets present these feelings?

WHAT TO LOOK FOR

Remember, you will need to **compare** and **contrast** the two poems. Think about the **similarities** and **differences** between:

- the poems' 'stories' and what is happening or has happened
- the themes – how inner thoughts and fears are depicted and what they tell you about the way the poet presents these fears
- most importantly, the language, form and voice the poets have chosen. (You will need to look for evidence and the techniques used and discuss their similarities or differences as well as their effects.)

TOP TIP ⭐

Don't write too many annotations. Remember, in the exam there are only 8 marks available for the comparison question.

① Keeping the question and bullet points in mind, make your own annotations comparing the two poems.

WRITING YOUR ANSWER

Here is one approach showing the beginning of a Good Level answer.

Paragraph	Main points	Example/evidence
Paragraph 1	Open by making a comment on a similarity or difference in 'story' and theme between the two poems.	*In contrast to 'The Call', 'Canto CCCLXIV' is not told like an allegory, but depicts a series of images. However, like 'The Call' it seems to be concerned with feelings of fear and anxiety. The image of the baby's sad 'wail' suggests the fears expressed in dreams that are instinctive 'primal … cries'. This is similar to the disturbing 'call' that the urgent voice makes in Mew's poem. It links to the speaker's inner fears about going out into an unknown bitter 'world'.*
Paragraph 2	Briefly discuss the language and its effects in both poems further. (For example, compare the many powerful verbs, adjectives and nouns and how they describe inner feelings and emotions.)	
Paragraph 3	Briefly compare/contrast the form, structure and speakers of the poems. (For example, 'Canto CCCLXIV' shifts direction in the second half to describe those who cannot express fears. Does 'The Call' shift in any way? If so, is it similar to or different from 'Canto CCCLXIV'?)	
Conclusion	Draw your answer to a conclusion by making a last point, using a suitable connective, such as 'Finally …'. Or you could sum up what you think is the most important similarity or difference.	

2 Using the plan above (or a plan of your own) write an answer to the question.

3 Now, for further practice, read the poem below and answer the question comparing it with 'Text' by Carol Ann Duffy on page 18.

comparing it with 'Text' by Carol Ann Duffy on page 18.

'This living hand, now warm and capable'

This living hand, now warm and capable

Of earnest grasping, would, if it were cold

And in the icy silence of the tomb,

So haunt thy days and chill thy dreaming nights

5   That thou would wish thine own heart dry of blood

So in my veins red life might stream again,

And thou be conscience-calm'd – see here it is –

I hold it towards you.

John Keats

> **TOP TIP**
>
> Remember, in the exam you will already have answered the first question in Section C, so you should already have an understanding of the first poem to draw on when you answer the second question.

QUESTION

In both 'Text' and 'This living hand, now warm and capable', the speakers describe their feelings about reaching out to another person. What are the similarities and/or differences between the ways the poets present these feelings?

PROGRESS CHECK

GOOD PROGRESS

I can:

- identify and explain clearly similarities and differences of language, form, voice and structure in two unseen poems. ☐
- support my comments with evidence from the unseen poems, refer to accurate terminology and show their effects. ☐

EXCELLENT PROGRESS

I can:

- identify and analyse similarities and differences between two unseen poems, giving insights into language, form, voice and structure. ☐
- make apt comments, selecting and analysing evidence from the two poems, and use subject terminology thoughtfully, describing its various effects. ☐

PART FOUR: SAMPLE PAPERS, ANSWERS AND PRACTICE TASKS

HOW TO USE THIS SECTION

This section will provide you with three sample responses to questions similar to Questions 1 and 2 from Paper 2, Section C: Unseen poetry.

These enable you to compare responses at a **Mid**, **Good** and **Very High** Level.

Once you have read the poem and the question that follows it, choose two sample responses to compare, based on the level you are currently at. You may choose to focus on responses that are at and above your own level, for example, Mid and Good Level; or Good and Very High Level.

TOP TIP ★

It is useful to read the sample responses aloud. It can give you a better impression of the style and pace of the writing. You may also find it useful to read with a partner and discuss the differences between the responses.

1 Read the **introduction** to each response and the **annotation** that accompanies it.

2 Identify the differences between the two introductions – what makes one better than the other.

3 Read through the rest of the two responses and annotations, noting **differences in style** and **improvements** that you can make to your own writing.

4 Read the **bullet points** to help you achieve a better level.

5 Now, try writing your own response to each Question, using the upper Level answer as your guide. Use the Mark scheme on page 59 to help you.

Here is an example of a comparison of two introductions.

Mid Level response (page 46)	Good Level response (page 48)	Improvements I can make
Uses 'is about'	Uses 'depicts'	Use more specific vocabulary
Tends to be monotonous. There are three sentences, all of similar pace and flow.	Has a short sentence followed by a long one, which creates a varied pace.	Vary sentence lengths
The repetition of 'The poem … is about' (sentences 1 and 3) in the Mid Level response adds to the monotony.	Uses a wide and varied vocabulary.	Avoid repeating words/groups of words

SAMPLE PAPER, QUESTION 1

Read the poem, then answer the question that follows it.

Piccadilly Line

Girls dressed for dancing,
board the tube at Earl's Court,
flutter, settle.
Chattering, excited by a vision
5 of glitter, their fragile bodies
carry invisible antennae,
missing nothing.
Faces velvet with bright camouflage,
they're unsung stars – so young
10 it's thrilling just to be away from home.

One shrieks, points, springs away.
She's seen a moth
caught up in the blonde strands
of her companion's hair,
15 a moth, marked
with all the shallow colours of blonde.
The friend's not scared;
gently she shakes her head,
tumbles it, dead,
20 into her hands.

At Piccadilly Circus they take flight,
skimming the escalator,
brushing past the collector,
up to the lure of light.

Carole Satyamurti

1 In 'Piccadilly Line', how does the poet present the speaker's feelings about what it means to be young?

[24 marks]

ANNOTATED SAMPLE ANSWERS

SAMPLE ANSWER A

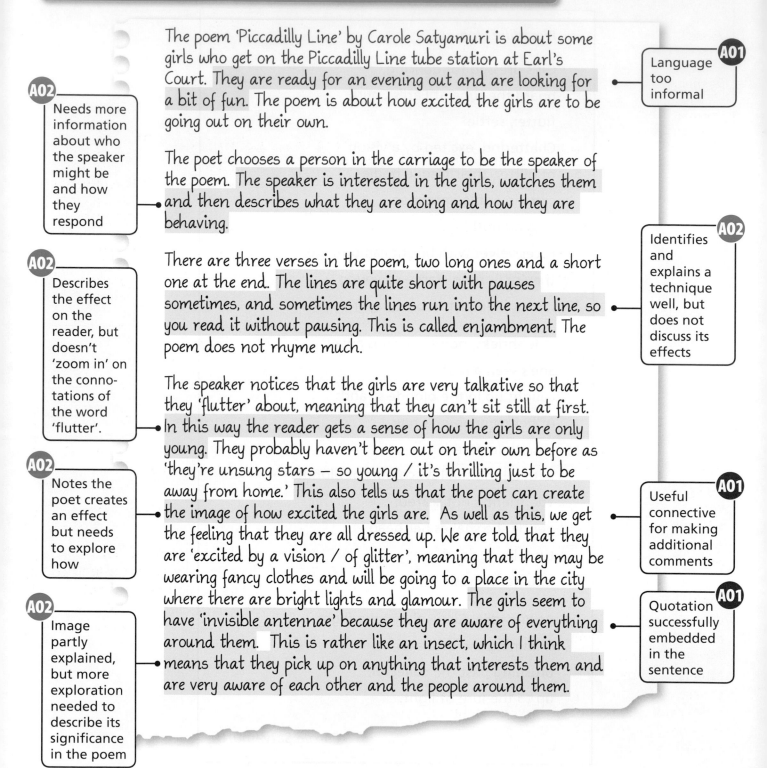

A02 Needs more information about who the speaker might be and how they respond

A02 Describes the effect on the reader, but doesn't 'zoom in' on the connotations of the word 'flutter'.

A02 Notes the poet creates an effect but needs to explore how

A02 Image partly explained, but more exploration needed to describe its significance in the poem

The poem 'Piccadilly Line' by Carole Satyamuri is about some girls who get on the Piccadilly Line tube station at Earl's Court. They are ready for an evening out and are looking for a bit of fun. The poem is about how excited the girls are to be going out on their own.

The poet chooses a person in the carriage to be the speaker of the poem. The speaker is interested in the girls, watches them and then describes what they are doing and how they are behaving.

There are three verses in the poem, two long ones and a short one at the end. The lines are quite short with pauses sometimes, and sometimes the lines run into the next line, so you read it without pausing. This is called enjambment. The poem does not rhyme much.

The speaker notices that the girls are very talkative so that they 'flutter' about, meaning that they can't sit still at first. In this way the reader gets a sense of how the girls are only young. They probably haven't been out on their own before as 'they're unsung stars – so young / it's thrilling just to be away from home.' This also tells us that the poet can create the image of how excited the girls are. As well as this, we get the feeling that they are all dressed up. We are told that they are 'excited by a vision / of glitter', meaning that they may be wearing fancy clothes and will be going to a place in the city where there are bright lights and glamour. The girls seem to have 'invisible antennae' because they are aware of everything around them. This is rather like an insect, which I think means that they pick up on anything that interests them and are very aware of each other and the people around them.

A01 Language too informal

A02 Identifies and explains a technique well, but does not discuss its effects

A01 Useful connective for making additional comments

A01 Quotation successfully embedded in the sentence

AO2

Sound links made between the images in the verses, but links should be explored further and effects of the images described

In the second verse one of the girls starts to 'shriek' and makes a fuss. This is because a moth gets caught up in her friend's hair, which is 'blonde' and the same colour as the moth. However, the friend isn't bothered by the moth. All she does is shake her head and the moth falls out. It is dead. The events about the moth in the second verse link back to the mention of the insect and its antennae in the first verse. Moths 'flutter' as well and so do the girls. So perhaps the poet is saying that the girls are like moths.

In the final verse, which is much shorter than the other two, the train arrives at Piccadilly Station and the girls get off. For example, the speaker says that they are 'skimming the escalator'. I suppose the poet is presenting the girls as moths again, because moths are attracted to light and the girls are also attracted to light. By this, I think the poet means that the girls are attracted to the lights of the city.

AO2

Needs to identify the technique (extended metaphor) used and explore it and its effects fully in the poem

MID LEVEL

Comment

There is a sound general grasp of the events in the poem and some understanding of implied meanings. Quotations are sometimes embedded in a sentence successfully, but a critical style of writing needs to be developed. There also needs to be a fuller exploration of what the poet is presenting to the reader and how the reader is affected. An understanding of the role of the speaker and of the form and style of the poem is also needed. Poetic techniques need to be identified and their effects discussed. For example, what might the extended metaphor of the moth mean in 'Piccadilly Line'? Could it represent more than one thing?

For a Good Level:

- Focus in on specific words, phrases and techniques and fully explain their effects.
- Support all comments with evidence from the poem.
- Develop a critical style: avoid informal language, learn to vary sentence length and pace, avoid repeating comments and increase vocabulary.

SAMPLE ANSWER B

A02 Speculates about the nature of the speaker but needs to provide some evidence or to show uncertainty about who the speaker is

Carole Satyamurti's 'Piccadilly Line' is written in free verse. It depicts young girls who are going out for the evening to enjoy themselves and who join the 'Piccadilly Line' at Earl's Court Station on the London Underground.

A01 Clear introduction that sums up what the poem is about

The girls are 'dressed for dancing' so are full of life and ready for fun and entertainment. The speaker of the poem is a passenger and probably an older woman, who notices them and watches what they do. The poet presents the girls through the eyes of the speaker, who understands the girls' excitement and their feelings about being 'away from home' and outside their parents' control.

A02 Identifies techniques related to form and shows their effects

The poem is written in three stanzas, the first two of ten lines and the last of four. The lines are almost all short and pacey. In this respect the rhythm is rather like the girls who chatter excitedly to each other. Sometimes the poet uses enjambment so that a line runs on into the next line and then pauses in the middle of a line (caesura). This seems to reinforce the sense that the girls are 'chattering' erratically, as we all do when we are excited.

A01 Useful connective to show time

A02 Quotations nicely embedded in the sentence

In the first stanza we are introduced to the girls. The poet chooses a powerful verb, 'flutter', in line three to describe their lively nature, as if their enthusiasm at the thought of being allowed out makes them unable to 'settle' down quickly into their seats. Another image, 'a vision / of glitter', conveys the bright lights of the city to which the girls are attracted. There are also images that suggest the girls are like moths. They have hidden 'antennae'. Moths use their antennae to tell them about their surroundings and in the same way the girls are very aware of their surroundings, because it is a new experience for them. The girls wear 'camouflage' on their faces, which is a metaphor for make-up. Moths are camouflaged as a disguise to blend into their surroundings and the girls also wear their make-up, the reader can assume, as a kind of disguise so they will look older. They are also attracted to the city lights in the way that moths are attracted to the light.

A02 Shows the effect of a poetic technique on the reader

A02

Identifies a technique and its purpose correctly but could explore even further the extended metaphor of the moth and its multiple meanings

In the second stanza there is a development when an incident involving a moth in the train carriage occurs. It is caught up in one of the girl's hair and, seeing it, her friend 'shrieks', but the girl is not afraid and she shakes the moth, which is dead, from her hair. Since the metaphor of the moth is used throughout the poem it is an extended metaphor that emphasises the importance of the moth as an image. So what else does it mean? Moths do not live very long, so perhaps it is a metaphor for the way in which the girls' youthfulness and energy will only last for a short time in their lives.

A01

Rhetorical question that enhances the style

In the last stanza, which is much shorter than the others, the girls leave the train at Piccadilly Circus station. The speaker imagines them 'skimming the escalator' and 'brushing past the collector', so it reminds us of the moth again. The mood of the poem is more light-hearted again, too. The girls are on their way to enjoy themselves in the city.

A01

A sound conclusion that identifies a shift in mood, but the point needs to be developed more fully

GOOD LEVEL

Comment

A good answer that shows a sound understanding of the feelings presented by the poet. Key features have been identified, such as language, form, structure and voice, but a greater exploration of their effects is needed. Poetic techniques have been highlighted, but sometimes evidence of effects is lacking. The critical style is competent and clear, and some useful techniques have been used, but the structure is rather repetitive and the pace also needs some variation. The conclusion is effective, but links with the earlier part of the poem could have been identified more clearly.

For a High Level:

- Make sure links are made between all the techniques mentioned and the effects the poet creates.
- Study the poet's techniques and effects more carefully for further, more complex insights.
- Vary the sentence structures in terms of length and pace to improve the critical style.
- Introduce more sophisticated vocabulary.

SAMPLE ANSWER C

A02 Excellent opening that identifies the poem's focus, the style of the poem and also highlights the speaker's position and concerns

In Carole Satyamurti's free verse poem, the speaker, a passenger on the London Underground's Piccadilly Line, notices two (or more) young women 'dressed for dancing' who 'board the tube at Earl's Court' station. Fascinated by their high spirits and inexperience, the speaker watches them interact and explores what it means to be young.

The speaker's voice depicts the girl's excited mood, noting that they are 'so young' they must feel 'it's thrilling just to be away from home'. We can assume, therefore, that the girls are teenagers allowed to enjoy an evening in the city and are experiencing a new-found freedom. The adjectival phrase 'so young' also implies that the speaker is older with a greater experience of life. Perhaps she is a woman, since she is able to empathise with the girls' female youthfulness?

A01 Quotations successfully embedded in the text

A01 Rhetorical question that enhances the style. Also, using 'perhaps' allows the student to speculate about who the speaker might be

A01 Useful connective used to qualify a point

The lines in all three stanzas are generally short and a line often runs on into the next line with a kind of breathlessness. However, the poet has also chosen to use caesura as well as enjambment, as if the speaker has to stop for breath, too. Determiners are sometimes left out. The first line begins 'Girls' Instead of 'Some girls' and verbs sometimes follow in quick succession as in 'shrieks, points, springs'. The poem is also told in the present tense, which gives it a sense of immediacy. All these techniques work together to mirror the excited 'Chattering' girls.

A02 Identifies a series of techniques related to form and shows their effects in a sophisti-cated way

A02 Points to the poet's choice of techniques

A02 Focuses on particular word choice and what it suggests

In the first stanza, while Carole Satyamurti presents a series of images that are associated with the girls' attraction to the bright city lights, an important metaphor is also introduced. The verb 'flutter' has connotations of something light and delicate, such as a winged creature, but when accompanied by the verb, 'settle', it suggests a moth. The metaphor is extended. The girls, alert to their surroundings, have 'invisible antennae / missing nothing'. A moth's antennae are sensitive to its surroundings. The girls wear make-up – 'a velvet ... camouflage', suggesting the moth's soft wings and ability to disguise its features, just as make-up can disguise someone's age. Most of all, like the moth, they are attracted to the light, 'a vision / of glitter'.

A02 Focuses in to analyse the effects of imagery

But the metaphor of the moth also implies that the girls are vulnerable. Their 'bodies' are 'fragile', like the moth's, reinforcing the idea that there is risk as well as adventure in the big city. The extended metaphor continues in stanza two and into the final stanza.

> A02
> Explores the extended metaphor of the moth to identify further meanings

> A02
> Important mention of structure and technique, showing how they work together and create more than one effect

The structure of the poem is also developed in stanza two when a dramatic moment is introduced. An actual moth is caught in one of the girl's blonde hair and her friend squeals in panic. The girl is unperturbed as she 'shakes her head' and the moth spills out, dead. The effect of this change in the structure, along with using an extended metaphor rather than a simple one, emphasises the moth's brief life. It allows the poet to give the idea greater power: to suggest that youth itself is a very brief, if intense, period of life.

The last stanza of the poem is short. It contrasts with the previous stanzas in length but returns to the mood of the first. For the reader, the full rhyme helps to bring a satisfying closure to the poem. The girls leave the carriage and 'take flight', like those moths that survive. For the moment their youthful optimism is what matters, as they ascend the escalator at Piccadilly Circus drawn to the 'lure' of the city.

> A01
> Excellent conclusion that makes appropriate links with the intro-duction

VERY HIGH LEVEL

Comment

This is an excellent analysis of the poem, which has a sustained focus on the question. The choice of vocabulary is very mature and the style and pace fluent and clear. All the poem's main features: language, form, structure and voice have been identified along with a thorough discussion of the poet's choice of techniques and their effects. The sophistication of some of the techniques, such as their dual effect, has not been missed. The conclusion is rounded off very well indeed and makes a neat connection with the introduction.

SAMPLE PAPER, QUESTION 2

Read both poems, then answer the question that follows them.

You have already answered Question 1 about 'Piccadilly Line'.

Piccadilly Line

Girls dressed for dancing,
board the tube at Earl's Court,
flutter, settle.
Chattering, excited by a vision
5 of glitter, their fragile bodies
carry invisible antennae,
missing nothing.
Faces velvet with bright camouflage,
they're unsung stars – so young
10 it's thrilling just to be away from home.

One shrieks, points, springs away.
She's seen a moth
caught up in the blonde strands
of her companion's hair,
15 a moth, marked
with all the shallow colours of blonde.
The friend's not scared;
gently she shakes her head,
tumbles it, dead,
20 into her hands.

At Piccadilly Circus they take flight,
skimming the escalator,
brushing past the collector,
up to the lure of light.

Carole Satyamurti

The Letter

from Gwyneth Benbow

I live her memory as if it were my own:
a path through woods and four girls racing down
– Gwyneth, Elen, Ceinwen, Vi – three sisters and a friend
whose letter out of the blue brought scent and sound
5   of a long ago spring day between the wars:

a river rippling of stones, laughter of girls,
skelter of skirts into the kitchen at Nant Mill.
Two older sisters set the great elm table,
loaves cool on a rack, churned butter gleams,
10   five handsome brothers tramp in from the fields.

All over the world a child's still running home
through grim street, grimy ginnel, field or slum.
Inside the old ones, ending their century,
the child who was, alive in memory,
15   and who they were, lover, mother, hero.

Some lose themselves and us before they go.
Some live as if they had all the time in the world
to brave out frailty and pain, still panning for gold.

Gillian Clarke

2 In both 'The Letter' and 'Piccadilly Line', the speakers describe feelings about youth and the passing of time. What are the similarities and/or differences between the way the poets present those feelings?

[8 marks]

ANNOTATED SAMPLE ANSWERS

SAMPLE ANSWER A

AO2 Shows a grasp of events and focus at the opening of the poem and draws similarities

'The Letter' by Gillian Clarke is similar to 'Piccadilly Line' in that it is about some young girls who are enjoying themselves, but it does not take place on a train. 'The Letter' takes place in the countryside near a place called 'Nant Mill'. The speaker of the poem in 'The Letter' receives a letter from a friend and a memory of a time they had together comes back.

AO2 A good attempt to understand the imagery

The girls in 'The Letter' are called, Gwyneth, Elen, Ceinwen and Vi. They are pictured running down a track towards 'Nant Mill' and going into the kitchen. They are like the girls in 'Piccadilly' line because they seem to be messing around. Their skirts, which are described in an image as a 'skelter of skirts', are flying, which tells us that they are happy and perhaps out of breath. In the kitchen some one has been baking bread, which is cooling 'on a rack'. There is butter too and five brothers arrive. I think It is a happy scene because all the people are young, the same as in 'Piccadilly Line', although the images there are of the city lights, so very different.

AO1 Language too informal

AO2 Needs to consider how and why the imagery is different

In 'Piccadilly Line' the setting stays in the railway carriage, but in the third verse of 'The Letter' the poet changes the scene. The girls have gone and instead there is a picture of other children across the world, although like the girls they are running too. But the children in the verse are poor because some are running home to a 'slum' or 'grim street' so perhaps the poet is saying that children wherever they come from are the same because they are young. At the end of the verse there is an image of old people, who remember 'the child who was' so are thinking back to when they were young too. In this way the poet is presenting the passing of time.

AO1 Quotations successfully embedded in the text

AO2 Identifies an important theme, but needs to explore it further and how it may link to other themes

The final verse is only three lines. It is different from 'Piccadilly Line' because it only includes the young girls, whereas in 'The Letter' the poet seems to be showing us how people age and the passing of time. Some people 'lose themselves and us', meaning that they do not keep in touch with their families and loved ones. Then there are others who do not worry about the future or about growing old.

AO2 Needs to consider the form and the mood of the stanza and its effects at the end of the poem

MID LEVEL

Comment

There is a reasonable grasp of the events in the two poems, the differences of setting and similarities of theme and some understanding of hidden meanings. The differences of imagery, some of which are identified, need to be explored further, commenting on the effects of the language. In the same way, how the poet uses other techniques needs to be investigated. Connectives of comparison and contrast are sometimes used. However, if a greater range were used along with a varied sentence structure, it would make the writing more concise and readable.

For a Good Level:

- Compare and contrast the poems more fully.
- Show how the poets use techniques to create different or similar effects.
- Avoid slang and informal language.
- Use a greater range of connectives, vary sentences, increase vocabulary and learn to adopt a critical style.

SAMPLE ANSWER B

AO2
A strong introduc-tion that draws similarities between themes and differences of setting

Gillian Clarke's poem has a similar theme to 'Piccadilly Line' since it is about lively young girls. However, in Gillian Clarke's poem the speaker receives a letter from a friend from long ago and she remembers an important memory. This contrasts with 'Piccadilly Line', which takes place on a train. The opening line of 'The Letter' tells the reader how vivid and happy the memory is as the speaker recalls it.

AO2
Focuses in to describe techniques and their effect. Notes similarities

In the first and second stanza the girls, Gwyneth, Elen, Ceinwen and Vi, are running down a path in woods and entering the kitchen at 'Nant Mill', which is probably a farm. Fresh loaves are baked and the butter 'gleams', so the mood is happy and the memory feels like an almost perfect one of youth. The poet presents an image of them wearing 'a skelter of skirts', as though they have been running so hard their skirts are flying everywhere; 'skelter' also reminds us of the 'helter skelter' that you slide down wildly at a theme park. In this respect the poem is similar to 'Piccadilly Line' where the girls are full of youthful fun.

AO2
Identifies an important theme, but needs to make a closer link between the passing of time and youth and how they are presented

In the third stanza the poem changes in mood. It becomes quite serious, whereas 'Piccadilly Line' stays upbeat. Gillian Clarke presents images of children across the world but they are mainly poor and 'running home / through grim street' or 'slum'. The verse then turns to the elderly and another theme, the passing of time. The elderly still remember their childhoods and 'who they were' because their memories are strong. The final stanza is a tercet and because it is short it seems to help bring the poem to a close.

AO1
Language inappropri-ate, too informal

AO2
A strong conclusion, but could mention more about the mood in both poems

In 'Piccadilly Line' the moth was an extended metaphor for the girls' youth because like the moth, youth does not last. In 'The Letter' the speaker thinks about what happens to us as we get older and die. Some of us 'lose' ourselves, which I think means that we may get ill or lose our family and friends. Others carry on without thinking much about time and age and perhaps do not prepare themselves for 'frailty and pain'.

GOOD LEVEL

Comment

Shows a good grasp of the two poems, though a few more similarities and differences could have been drawn out. Several literary techniques have been discussed and some in-depth analysis has been attempted. Key points have been made about theme and language and a shift in the structure of the second poem has been noted. More analysis of form, mood and voice would be useful. The style is generally fluent and appropriate connectives have been used, but the critical style could be developed further.

For a High Level:

- Look for further similarities and differences between the poems.
- Aim for a greater in-depth analysis of some techniques to reveal their effects.
- Try to condense some of the points being made and include some shorter sentences to improve the pace.
- Avoid slang and informal language.

SAMPLE ANSWER C

A01
Excellently written, concise opening that focuses on theme

Like 'Piccadilly Line', one main theme of 'The Letter' is youth and its high spirits. However, in contrast to 'Piccadilly Line', in which the speaker is unknown to the girls, Gillian Clarke's poem opens with a memory from the distant past. It is sparked by an unexpected letter from an old friend. The opening line addresses the reader directly. It also feels as if the speaker is thinking aloud as the past returns with a rush. The voice is surprised, but joyous as the 'memory' is relived.

A02
Points to a line as evidence and gives a well-considered view of the voice

'Piccadilly Line' has an urban setting and most of the imagery is of the city, but in the first two quintains of 'The Letter' the setting is a rural one and nature imagery is used. A group of girls are running down 'a path through woods' one 'spring day' to arrive at a farmhouse kitchen. The verb 'rippling' suggests the girls' waves of 'laughter' as much as the image of the nearby river. The same energy is conveyed through the image 'skelter of skirts'. It has associations with the expression 'helter-skelter' (meaning speed and confusion), and also through the use of the sibilant as we imagine the girls' skirts' flapping back and forth as they run.

A02
Focuses in to examine key techniques and their effects

A02
Successfully identifies contrasting setting and types of imagery in the poems

By the third quintain the poem shifts dramatically. The pattern of the lines and stanzas remains the same, but the mood becomes much more serious than in 'Piccadilly Line'. However, like the latter, there are references to the city, if not to its bright lights. Instead, the city images are of children across the world, still with youthful energy, 'running home' but through 'grim street' and 'grimy ginnel'. The sense of poverty is reinforced here by alliteration in the hard, heavy-sounding 'g'. Youth is then depicted in the elderly, as 'the child who was' and who is still alive through memories, despite the passing of time.

A01
Well constructed sentence that uses connectives to qualify and compare and also points to a contrast

A01
An eloquent expression of change of mood

A01
Useful connective of contrast

A02
Successful attempt to explain the effect of alliteration

The final stanza of 'The Letter' is a tercet and, as with 'Piccadilly Line', is a short stanza that contains rhyme, bringing the poem to a neat close. Carole Satyamurti presents the theme of youth's brief life through the extended metaphor of the 'moth', but ends on an optimistic note. Gillian Clarke chooses a different mood and a less optimistic one to present time passing. Touching images depict the way different lives turn out. There are those who suffer misfortune and breakdown so that they 'lose themselves and us' and there are those who think nothing of time and its consequences, who still trust in luck, as the final metaphor 'panning for gold' implies.

A02
Excellent conclusion that contrasts the poems' different moods but makes a link to their themes

Comment

An excellent response to the question. The student gives a sophisticated comparison of the two poems, weaving descriptions of similarities and differences through each paragraph. The main features, voice, form and language have been discussed along with theme and mood. An examination has been made of a variety of techniques and their effects. The style is fluent with a variety of sentence structures, pace and vocabulary enhancing the points being made.

ASSESS YOURSELF

Use the following Mark scheme as a guide to decide what level you are.

Level	First poem	Both poems
Very High	• You show a full understanding and a sound analysis of the poem, and present a well-structured argument. • Your references are carefully chosen and you comment on language, form and structure with perception and the appropriate use of poetic techniques, pointing to the effects they create.	• You compare the poems, showing a sophisticated awareness of their similarities and differences. • You describe the effects of the writer's approach on the reader to a high degree, using perceptive analysis and appropriate references.
Good	• You show a good understanding of the poem and write clearly and thoughtfully. • You make sound references and refer to poetic techniques, including them appropriately in your response.	• You draw out the important similarities and differences showing some degree of sophistication relating to language, form and structure. • You identify the effects the writer creates, making suitable references that are integrated into the writing.
Mid	• You show clear understanding of the poem and use references appropriately. • You explain the writer's methods clearly and show understanding of some of the effects on the reader.	• You make some relevant comparisons in terms of language, form and structure. • You are able to explain some of the different effects the writer creates.

PRACTICE PAPER 1

Complete this practice paper. It consists of two unseen poems and two questions – just like Paper 2, Section C: Unseen poetry in your exam. Use the tips below to help you answer the questions.

Remember, allow yourself at least 45 minutes to answer questions on the unseen poems.

Moving

Moving in, I think I thought
that here was a house
in which our troubled souls
might one day come to rest.
5   Nothing in the street seemed planned,
each house a blueprint of the grand.

But there were omens from the start.
Our hired van came late –
stock full of toys, your clothes, our books,
10   the tired ten year wedding gifts which
symbolized our disappointment.

Walking for milk to lace our tea
I passed another scene of change.
In a front room behind a bay she stood alone
15   contemplating a vacancy.
Her parents and her kids standing at the door,
the cases lined like gravestones in the hall.

When it came, the day I left that place,
I thought of this, how she'd watch me pass,
20   her empty eyes, the rawness of her face,
how it seemed to stand for something
pre-determined, a truth about life,
each of us alone, an empty space.

                                    John Pownall

---

1 In 'Moving', how does the poet present the speaker's feelings about what it means to move home?

                                              [24 marks]

TOP TIP

Follow the sequence for reading and annotating the poem as you learned about on pages 8 and 17. Then write your response, using your annotations where appropriate.

Abandoned Farmhouse

He was a big man, says the size of his shoes
on a pile of broken dishes by the house;
a tall man too, says the length of the bed
in an upstairs room; and a good, God-fearing man,
5   says the Bible with a broken back
on the floor below the window, dusty with sun;
but not a man for farming, say the fields
cluttered with boulders and the leaky barn.

A woman lived with him, says the bedroom wall
10   papered with lilacs and the kitchen shelves
covered with oilcloth, and they had a child,
says the sandbox made from a tractor tire.
Money was scarce, say the jars of plum preserves
and canned tomatoes sealed in the cellar hole.
15   And the winters cold, say the rags in the window frames.
It was lonely here, says the narrow country road.

Something went wrong, says the empty house
in the weed-choked yard. Stones in the fields
say he was not a farmer; the still-sealed jars
20   in the cellar say she left in a nervous haste.
And the child? Its toys are strewn in the yard
like branches after a storm – a rubber cow,
a rusty tractor with a broken plow,
a doll in overalls. Something went wrong, they say.

Ted Kooser

2 In both 'Moving' and 'Abandoned Farmhouse' the speakers describe feelings about empty or abandoned homes. What are the similarities and/or differences between the ways the poets present those feelings?

[8 marks]

TOP TIP

Follow the sequence for reading and annotating the second poem as you learned about on page 29. Then write your response, using your annotations where appropriate.

PRACTICE PAPER 2

Complete this practice paper. It consists of two unseen poems and two questions. Write a full response as though you were in the exam. You might like to time how long you take. You can use the tips provided for Practice Paper 1 to help you approach these questions too.

Sally

She was a dog-rose kind of girl:
elusive, scattery as petals;
scratchy sometimes, tripping you like briars.
She teased the boys
5 turning this way and that, not to be tamed
or taught any more than the wind.
Even in school the word 'ought'
had no meaning for Sally.
On dull days
10 she'd sit quiet as a mole at her desk
delving in thought.
But when the sun called
she was gone, running the blue day down
till the warm hedgerows prickled the dusk
15 and moths flickered out.

Her mother scolded; Dad
gave her the hazel switch,
said her head was stuffed with feathers
and a starling tongue.
20 But they couldn't take the shine out of her.
Even when it rained
you felt the sun saved under her skin.
She'd a way of escape
laughing at you from the bright end of a tunnel,
25 leaving you in the dark.

Phoebe Hesketh

1 In 'Sally', how does the poet present the speaker's feelings about Sally?

[24 marks]

She dwelt among the untrodden ways

She dwelt among the untrodden ways
Beside the springs of Dove,
A Maid whom there were none to praise
And very few to love:

5   A violet by a mossy stone
Half hidden from the eye!
– Fair as a star, when only one
Is shining in the sky.

She lived unknown, and few could know
10 When Lucy ceased to be;
But she is in her grave, and, oh,
The difference to me!

William Wordsworth

---

2 In both 'Sally' and 'She dwelt among the untrodden ways' the speakers
describe feelings about people they admire or love. What are the
similarities and/or differences between the way the poets present those
feelings?

[8 marks]

PRACTICE PAPER 3

Complete this final practice paper. It consists of two unseen poems and two questions. Set a timer for 45 minutes and write a full response in the time allowed. Try to remember the tips on pages 60–1 and only refer to them if you get stuck!

Returning, We Hear the Larks

Sombre the night is:
And though we have our lives, we know
What sinister threat lies there.

Dragging these anguished limbs, we only know
5   This poison-blasted track opens on our camp –
On a little safe sleep.

But hark! Joy – joy – strange joy.
Lo! Heights of night ringing with unseen larks:
Music showering on our upturned listening faces.

10 Death could drop from the dark
As easily as song;
But song only dropped,
Like a blind man's dreams on the sand
By dangerous tides;
15 Like a girl's dark hair, for she dreams no ruin lies there,
Or her kisses where a serpent hides.

Isaac Rosenberg

---

1 In 'Returning, We Hear the Larks', how does the poet present the speaker's feelings about nature and war?

[24 marks]

In Hospital

Under the shadow of a hawthorn brake,
Where bluebells draw the sky down to the wood,
Where, 'mid brown leaves, the primroses awake
And hidden violets smell of solitude;
5   Beneath green leaves bright-fluttered by the wing
Of fleeting, beautiful, immortal Spring,
I should have said, 'I love you,' and your eyes
Have said, 'I, too ...' The gods saw otherwise.

For this is winter, and the London streets
10   Are full of soldiers from that far, fierce fray
Where life knows death, and where poor glory meets
Full-face with shame, and weeps and turns away.
And in the broken, trampled foreign wood
Is horror, and the terrible scent of blood,
15   And love shines tremulous, like a drowning star,
Under the shadow of the wings of war.

Edith Nesbit

2 In both 'Returning, We Hear the Larks' and 'In Hospital' the speakers describe feelings about war and nature. What are the similarities and/or differences between the ways the poets present those feelings?

[8 marks]

LITERARY TERMS

allegory	a story, poem or work of art that has a hidden meaning, often with a moral
alliteration	repetition of the same sound in a stretch of language, usually at the beginning of words
ambiguity	when words or sentences have more than one meaning and it is not clear which is the true interpretation
assonance	the repetition of the same vowel sound in a stretch of language
ballad	a traditional story written in rhyme
caesura	a pause in a line of poetry that affects the pace and rhythm
colloquial	the everyday speech used by people in ordinary situations
connotation	an additional meaning attached to a word in specific circumstances, i.e. what it suggests or implies
consonance	the repetition of the same consonant sound in a stretch of language
couplet	two lines of poetry that are paired
enjambment	in poetry when a line runs on into the next line without pause, so carrying the sense through with it. Sometimes called a run-on line
extended metaphor	in poetry, a metaphor that continues some aspect of the image; it may continue into the next line or throughout the poem (See metaphor)
form	the way the poem is laid out on the page. (It can refer to a specific verse form or a specific type of poem, such as a shape poem or a sonnet. If a poem has no regular form it is usually called free verse.)
free verse	a form of poetry; verses without regular rhythm or pattern, though they may contain some patterns, such as rhyme or repetition
half-rhyme	where the rhyme at the end of a line has the same consonants but not the same vowel sound, so not quite a full rhyme e.g. pet/pat
iambic pentameter	a line of poetry consisting of five feet, each consisting of a weak syllable followed by a strong one
iambic tetrameter	a line of poetry consisting of four feet, each consisting of a weak syllable followed by a strong one
iambic trimeter	a line of poetry consisting of three feet, each consisting of a weak syllable followed by a strong one
imagery	descriptive language that uses images to make actions, objects and characters more vivid in the reader's mind
metaphor	when one thing is used to describe another to create a striking or unusual image
metre	the pattern of stressed and unstressed syllables in a line of verse
mood	the tone or atmosphere created by an artistic work
narrative	a story
octave	a verse of eight lines, usually in iambic pentameter; the first eight lines of a sonnet (where it is sometimes called two quatrains)

persona	a character or strong voice adopted by the writer as the speaker
personificaton	the treatment or description of an object or idea as though they were human, with human feelings and attributes
perspective	the point of view from which a poem or work of fiction is written
quatrain	a **stanza** of four lines
rhetorical (question)	asked for effect rather than for an answer
rhyme scheme	the pattern of rhyme in a poem
rhyming couplet	a couplet that rhymes (See **couplet**)
sestet	a verse of six lines
sibilant	a hissing sound in speech made with an 's', 'ss', 'sh' or 'z'
simile	when one thing is compared directly with another using 'like' or 'as'
sonnet	a fourteen-line verse with a **rhyming couplet** at the end
stanza	a group or pattern of lines forming a verse
structure	the pattern, order or organisation of language and ideas and how they develop and change throughout the poem
tercet	a **stanza** of three lines
theme	the idea or ideas running through a poem or work of fiction
voice	the speaker or narrator of a poem or work of fiction. This **persona** is created in the speaker's mind, though sometimes it can seem close to the poet's or writer's own voice

ANSWERS

PART TWO

Voice and perspective (page 20)

1. Examples of further annotations that could be added:

- 'puppet' in line 9: a word a child might use
- 'Does he see me?' line 21: sense of childlike eagerness/excitement in the question?

2. The tone of the voice shifts particularly in lines 21–23, becoming hopeful at the thought that the salamander might become a friend, so that the mood of the poem shifts. (For a fuller answer see 3 below.)

3. The paragraphs could cover the following:

- The use of the first person perspective makes the voice seem more personal and direct.
- The present tense creates a sense of immediacy.
- Initially the voice sounds sad and suggests the child as well as the salamander is 'Searching' for friendship. Also, 'lonely' emphasises the child's solitude; but as he/she explores the salamander's world the voice sounds fascinated, entertained (e.g 'He is a clown', 'a shadow puppet') until at the end it becomes hopeful at the prospect of companionship (e.g. 'the colour of friendship').

Form and structure (page 22)

1. Examples of further annotations that could be added:

- No real rhyme or sound pattern – why?
- 'pressed / Under' end of line 9: Enjambment carries the idea of the leaf being caught and trapped
- 'Now', beginning of line 11: Change here? Up to now just what poet sees in life. Now – art?
- seventh couplet: Effects? Tells us that life is harder, more painful than art?
- final line: About reality not art, I think

2. Answers could include:

- The couplets are separate from one another and create a set of separate images about objects (for example) in different situations.
- The couplet reminds us of a series of pictures or photographs in a gallery.
- In couplets eight and nine there is a move away from separate images to a commentary on life rather than art. Life is more painful.

3. The paragraphs could cover the following:

- First five couplets depict common objects or creatures from urban life as stark images that are dead (the 'fox'), impaired (the 'trolley', 'door', 'gate'), trapped (the 'leaf'). The mood is solemn, disturbing.
- In the sixth stanza the images become those of conflict or destruction (e.g. the tank) and are also either photographs (images caught through the camera 'lens', such as a war photographer's, it is implied) or paintings (e.g. a 'mural').
- In the eighth stanza the images shift to the personal and are about reality, 'our' lives not art.
- The ninth stanza shows how for some (e.g. a 'child' somewhere) their reality is one of war and conflict. The 'thunder' of bombs is implied.

Language (page 24)

1. Examples of further annotations that could be added:

- 'long broken / path slabs': built urban environment contrasts with the natural fish – suggests decay versus wholesomeness?

2. Answers could include:

- Alliteration sibilant in lines 6–8: 'ci' and repeated 'sh' and 's' appeal to the sense of taste (its freshness), reinforcing the idea of a meal

3. Answers could include:

- Poem opens with the speaker thinking about the comfort of a meal after a long day's work, so that 'it is enough' stresses the need to focus on the meal alone.
- The alliteration on 'f' helps create a sense of the fish's wholesomeness and freshness, appeals to the appetite and conveys how much the speaker looks forward to the meal (as in 'fish', 'fresh', 'from' and 'fishmongers').
- The image 'to high / hurdle' and 'a sprinter's dinner' are sporting images. The first a powerful verb suggests an athlete racing/hurdling. The second is a metaphor for food eaten quickly, and along with 'a devil's rush' gives the reader a vivid impression of a stressful working life.

Worked task (page 26)

1. Examples of further annotations that could be added:

Speaker's feelings about love:

- love is universal (e.g. 'common as grass')
- its power (e.g. 'bury a bombsite, split asphalt')

- its persistence (e.g. 'grow / In any ditch, niche, or gutter')

The elderly man's thoughts about love:

- memories of his wife before her illness (e.g. 'soon her face / Will laugh in the mirror'; a princess not nineteen')
- memories are sacred (expressed through Sunday 'ritual tea' and the house as a 'shrine')

Speaker's feelings about the funeral:

Love and death through the extended metaphor of nature:

- memorable ('legend of her funeral')
- snowfall changes the scene (e.g. 'a swift wing / Of snow … transfigured all')
- healing power of nature (e.g. 'merciful as snow')
- love and nature together ('Love is like that … / Bandaging the bruised earth, white making the green grow.)

Conclusion: Comment on how themes of love and death come together in the two final stanzas through the extended metaphor of nature.

Form: Narrative in repeating octaves and regular rhythm and rhyme allow the story and speaker's thoughts to slowly unfold.

Voice: Reflective voice allows present thoughts (about past events and memories) to be explored (e.g. 'This much I learn').

2. Answers will vary.

PART THREE

Similarities (page 32)

Points you could make about the similarities between 'Abra-Cadabra' and 'Lineage':

- Walker presents the grandmother characters as 'strong' women who had a connection with nature through working on the land. Similarly, Nichols presents the 'mother' as a woman with knowledge of plants, such as 'the dark-green senna brew' and other herbal medicines.
- Walker presents the grandmothers as wise women who spoke 'many clean words', creating the impression that they had a commanding presence and gave useful advice from their experience of life. Similarly, Nichol's presents the mother as a 'magician' skilled in persuading her children to take their medicine by weaving 'incredible stories'.

- In both poems, memory and history are important themes as well as female relations. In 'Lineage' the grandmothers 'were full of memories', which we can read as family history. It also implies that memory is important to the speaker since the grandmothers left such a powerful impression. In 'Abracadabra' the mention of 'history' in the last line suggests not only the successful ending to the event with the 'pea' but also the speaker's memory of her past.
- Through the depiction of the grandmothers or the mother, the reader feels that both poets are presenting an awareness that an ancient knowledge (of domestic life, the natural world, family wisdom) is passed down through the female line.

Differences (page 36)

Points you could make about the differences between 'Drummer Hodge' and 'The Soldier':

- Brooke presents the speaker as patriotic, someone who thinks it is noble to die for one's country in war. Hardy, in contrast, presents a speaker who sees life as cheap in war.
- For the speaker, the 'foreign field' where he may be buried becomes, metaphorically, 'England'. In contrast, Hodge becomes part of the soil of the 'unknown plain', his home, implying England does not care about his death.
- Brooke presents England as perfection, a rural ideal (e.g. the effect of the image 'her flowers … her ways to roam' that is 'blest' (by God) is to create England as a perfect country). Hardy presents Hodge's home as a resting place 'unknown' to him, a place where the stars above are 'strange-eyed constellations'.
- The form differs between the poems. 'The Soldier' is a sonnet, written separately in two stanzas, as an octave followed by a sestet. The sonnet, a traditional love poem, suits the speaker's love of his country. 'Drummer Hodge' has three sestets, with repeated stanza and lines lengths and a regular rhythm. The formal nature suggests a funeral song (dirge) for the dead drummer boy.

Worked task (page 40)

1. Examples of further annotations that could be added:

Similarities:

- Language: Both use images of the unconscious. 'The Call': e.g. 'A flame within us'; 'Canto CCCLXIV'; e.g. 'primal mammalian cries'
- Form: both use rhyme; both use caesura and enjambment

Differences:

- Language: 'The Call': supernatural images: 'bright or dark angel'; 'Canto CCCLXIV': images of the everyday: 'a random living room'
- Form: 'The Call': allegory/narrative poem with irregular rhyme scheme; 'Canto CCCLXIV': free verse with regular rhyme and half-rhyme
- Structure: 'The Call': three stages: the interior, the call, going out into the world; 'Canto CCCLXIV': in the first nine lines images of cries and sounds, turning point in line ten, followed by nine lines of images of people unable to express fears
- Voice: 'The Call': storyteller voice, first person plural, past tense moving to present tense; 'Canto CCCLXIV': intimate voice through present tense third person

2. Answers will vary.

3. Examples of points you could have made:

Similarities:

- Both poets use an object to help express the idea of reaching out – for Duffy it is the mobile phone the speaker holds, whereas for Keats it is the speaker's own hand which he holds out. In both cases, the idea of hands, of touch, is important in reaching out to the other person.
- Both poems suggest an obsessive element to the feelings they describe – Duffy's speaker repeatedly 're-reads' the texts from her lover, whereas Keats's speaker imagines haunting the 'days' and 'nights' of the person he addresses.

Differences:

- The tone of Duffy's poem is forlorn – the simile of holding the phone like an 'injured bird' suggests the speaker's wounded feelings. The negative phrase 'Nothing ... will ever' implies that the relationship has broken down irrevocably.
- Keats's poem is sinister in tone and the speaker seems more in control. It is unclear whether the speaker is addressing a lover or the reader (does the 'hand' symbolise marriage or the poet himself?) but the speaker imagines his 'cold ... icy' fingers reaching out from beyond the grave, suggesting immortality.

PART FOUR

Practice paper 1 (page 60)

Question 1

Points you could have made:

AO1:

- Feelings of hope: new home would improve speaker's relationship

- Feelings of disappointment: signs of a continued failed relationship – soon after moving a sense of doubt sets in
- Feelings of sadness: speaker leaves the home
- Feelings of loneliness: speaker is reminded of an image of a lonely woman

AO2 Show how the poet presents:

- Use/effects of imagery of the house: e.g. a place where 'troubled souls / might one day come to rest' suggests, initially, the house as a place of healing; 'a blueprint of the grand' suggests a well-built, comfortable house that might be beneficial to the relationship
- Use/effects of imagery of speaker's relationship with partner/wife: e.g. 'the tired ten year wedding gifts' is an 'omen' suggesting disappointment with the relationship, which the new house cannot counteract; simile 'the cases lined like gravestones in the hall' implies that the speaker's relationship, like the gravestones, is marked by failure and has died
- Form: the poem is free verse, written in irregular stanzas, mainly sestets, which mirrors the changing thoughts of the speaker about the relationship and its decline. Irregular rhyme patterns are included, but in the last stanza there is a regular rhyme pattern: a,b,a,c,d,a, which helps to draw the poem to a strong conclusion emphasising a 'truth about life'.
- Use of structure to create the sense of decline in the relationship, despite the new home. First stanza begins hopefully, that relationship might mend, the new home might provide 'rest'; but early on (second stanza) there are 'omens', irritations that signify difficulties, e.g. 'van came late'; third stanza becomes a powerful metaphor for the death of the relationship, in the image of a woman at a window 'contemplating a vacancy', suggesting absence. Final stanza depicts the speaker's leave-taking and the separation from the relationship and the home, and the memory of the woman 'alone' at the window, suggesting that the home as well as the speaker is an 'an empty space'.
- Effects of last line: speaker recognises/contemplates that we are all separate, alone in life.

Question 2

AO2 Any valid comparisons, for example:

Similarities:

- Themes: both poems are metaphors for difficulties in family life /relationships and loss. In 'Abandoned Farmhouse' there is the sudden mysterious disappearance of family. In 'Moving' a dying relationship is played out in the house, which represents the decline of the relationship and the house's inability to mend it.

- Imagery: in 'Abandoned Farmhouse' the image of the 'empty house' reinforces the sense of abandonment. In 'Moving' the image 'contemplating a vacancy' reinforces the speaker's sense of loss of the relationship. The sad, cynical reference to 'that place' also suggests the house never became a home.

- Form: Both poems are free verse. Like 'Moving', 'Abandoned Farmhouse' uses rhyme to help close the poem, the couplet, 'cow' 'plow' highlights the final words.

Differences:

- Speaker in 'Abandoned Farmhouse' is an investigator's voice (similar to a detective) looking for clues about who lived in the house. The voice is distanced, unknown to the family. (See also personification below.) In contrast, speaker in 'Moving' is intimate, close to events, describing his/her feelings (e.g. 'I think I thought').

- Personification: In contrast to 'Moving', the house and its objects or features in 'Abandoned Farmhouse' are personified. The speaker reports to the reader what the features of the house reveal (e.g. 'He was a big man, says the size of his shoes').

- Form: While both poems are free verse, 'Abandoned Farmhouse' has a more regular stanza pattern (octaves). This reinforces the idea of building a picture of who lived there from clues, like a jigsaw puzzle.

- Images: In 'Abandoned Farmhouse', detailed images of the house and its features build an overall image of who lived there. Poverty is implied (e.g. 'rags in the window frames'). Implication is that the man who lived there 'was not a farmer' so 'Money was scarce' and the family left. By contrast, in 'Moving' there are few images of the house, only that it is comfortable and suburban. (See answers to Question 1.)

- Poems' endings: In 'Abandoned Farmhouse' there is no complete answer to the mystery of why the family left, 'Something went wrong' is the conclusion. In Contrast, 'Moving' has strong closure. (See answers to Question 1.)

Practice paper 2 (page 62)

Question 1

Points you could have made:

AO1:

- Feelings of amazement: Sally's quick, impulsive nature, sharpness, unpredictability

- Feelings of admiration: Sally's fearlessness, love of life, rebelliousness

- Feelings of respect: Sally's independence, lack of convention

- Feelings of fascination: Sally's contrariness: her wildness and elusiveness yet capacity for deep thought

AO2 Show how the poet presents:

- Use/effects of imagery to present Sally (e.g. similes 'dog-rose kind of girl', 'scattery as petals'; 'scratchy sometimes' suggests both her elusiveness and her prickly, sharp nature associated with a rose's thorns)

- Use and effects of other imagery that reveal: her ability to concentrate (e.g. 'a mole at her desk / delving in thought' has associations with deep thought, under the earth, as does the downward sound of the 'd' alliteration).

- Use of the sibilant 's' in 'scolded', 'hazel switch', reinforces the swish of the stick

- Use of form and structure to help create a sense of Sally's character. The poem is free verse in form, has pace, uses frequent enjambment (e.g. '"ought" / had no meaning for Sally') so that lines run on, usually reflecting Sally's quick, rebellious nature. But enjambment is also used to carry a thought on, slowing the pace with longer lines when Sally sits 'quiet as a mole at her desk / delving in thought'

- Use of nature imagery: 'warm hedgerows' has associations with warmth and summer, suggesting that Sally is warm and natural but also has a 'starling tongue', not afraid to say what she thinks or show objection

- Effects of last line: Sally's character is so bright, spirited and elusive that everyone else seems dull by comparison

Question 2

AO2 Any valid comparisons:

Similarities:

- Both poets present positive images of the poems' subjects. The speakers express love/admiration. In Wordsworth's poem, Lucy's death makes a huge 'difference' to the speaker's life. In Hesketh's poem, the speaker expresses admiration for Sally's love of life, 'they couldn't take the shine out of her'.

- Both poets use nature imagery. In Wordsworth's poem, Lucy is a 'violet', while Sally is compared to a 'dog-rose', conjuring images of unaffected, unsophisticated girls.

- Both poems have strong endings and closure. (See Answers to Question 1 for 'Sally'). The last line of 'She dwelt among the untrodden ways' conveys the speaker's profound remorse at Lucy's death.

Differences:

- Though both subjects are dear to the speaker, Sally in Hesketh's poem, is well known locally, is a memorable figure (e.g. is presented in different situations: in class, teasing 'boys', at home being scolded). By contrast, Lucy in Wordsworth's poem is unknown, moves in 'untrodden' circles.

- Imagery: Sally is attractive, mercurial (e.g. 'scattery as petals'). By contrast, Lucy is not conventionally pretty (e.g. 'Fair as a star, when only one / Is shining in the sky' suggests most would not find her attractive). However, 'Fair as a star' suggests that for the speaker she is attractive. Sally is lively, confident. Lucy is shy: like the violet she is 'Half hidden from the eye'.

- Form: While 'Sally' is free verse with largely fast-paced movement (see answers to Question 1), 'She dwelt among the untrodden ways' has only three short-lined, rhymed quatrains that mirror Lucy's lack of consequence/fame, but also provide a simple tribute from the speaker who loved her.

Practice paper 3 (page 64)

Question 1

Points you could have made:

AO1:

- Feelings of fear from enemy's attack (they are alive, but the threat is always present)

- Feelings of fatigue and the promise of a temporary respite when they sleep

- Feelings of happiness and surprise at the sound of larks

- Feelings that, like those on dangerous sands, death is as likely as joy

AO2: Show how the poet presents:

- Structure: The first two stanzas deal with the constant threat of death, even where they walk ('poison-blasted' suggests poison gas from bombs); the third stanza surprises with the sound of the birds, while the fourth reflects on the effect of the birdsong and the hidden menace in the skies.

- Voice: The use of the first person 'we' places the speaker in the trenches, and suggests a communal sharing of tiredness and fear with his comrades.

- Language: The choice of adjectives emphasises the hidden danger: 'sombre' and 'sinister' – dark and threatening. The sudden short exclamations convey the speaker's happiness: the repeated 'Joy', the emphatic 'Lo', suggest the men stopped in their tracks.

- Sound: The use of assonance in 'heights of night', contrasting with the 'Lo' (an intentional pun on 'low'?) create a singsong feel like the singing birds.

- Imagery: e.g. music 'showering' suggesting an almost physical sense of the song falling on the men, cleansing them.

- Reversal: In the final stanza the two comparisons return to the fear and danger – a blindman on sands with 'dangerous tides' suggests being caught out by not seeing the danger – like the bombs that might suddenly fall.

- Allusion: The image of the girl with the 'dark hair' who kisses the 'serpent' alludes to the idea of Eve's innocence in the Garden of Eden, and links back to the poison of the bombing.

Question 2

AO2 Any valid comparisons, for example:

Similarities:

- Voice: Both poems are told in the first person and touch on the terrible effects of war.

- Theme: In both poems, nature is presented as a positive force. In the first, the larks bring unexpected joy to the soldiers as they return. In the second, 'beautiful … Spring' recalls a time before or away from war near a 'hawthorn brake'.

- Theme: Both poems comment on the horrors of war: in the first, the 'poison-blasted track' and the potential for death to 'drop' from the sky emphasises the danger. In the second, the wood is 'broken' and 'trampled' and there is the 'terrible scent of blood.'

- Imagery: Both poems use figurative ideas to represent war and its effects – the drowning blindman on the beach representing the soldier is similar to 'love' in the second which is a 'drowning star.'

Differences:

- The second poem is directed to a particular person and is a reflection not just on the effects of war, but regrets about not expressing love for each other ('I should have said, "I love you,"'). Nature is used to recall a memory, a moment that was not grasped.

- The second poem also seems to take place in London, with war depicted through the contrasting 'wood' in each case – the destroyed one overseas, and the one from memory. The first poem is a single moment in the trenches, presumably overseas.

- The second poem is split into two stanzas, and the contrast comes between spring, the first stanza, and winter, the second. The first poem's contrasts are not to do with time but between the joy and despair of war and nature, and how love is drowned by the horrors of war. The speaker is also not directly involved in war but reminded of it by 'soldiers from that far, fierce fray'.

- The second poem also conveys a precise description of spring, with the 'violets', 'bluebells' and 'brown leaves' all building the picture, though the opening use of the word 'shadow' of the hawthorn hedge hints at the negative images to come.